ORTHODOXY AND
THE KINGDOM OF SATAN

FATHER SPYRIDON BAILEY

ORTHODOXY AND
THE KINGDOM OF SATAN

FATHER SPYRIDON BAILEY

FaR

Published in 2017 by FeedARead.com Publishing.
Financed by The Arts Council of Great Britain
Copyright © Father Spyridon Bailey

We know that we are of God, and that the whole world lies in the power of the evil one.
1 John 5 v19

Again, the devil took Him to a very high mountain and showed Him all the kingdoms of the world and their glory; and he said to Him, "All these things I will give you, if you fall down and worship me."
Matthew 4 v8-9

The ruler of this world has been judged.
John 16 v11

Contents

Introduction

In the late 1980s I read a book called *Orthodoxy And The Religion Of The Future*, written by Hieromonk Father Seraphim Rose. It was produced in the early 1970s, and deals with the growing influence on American culture of the New Age Movement. The book concludes that there is an intention to establish a single world religion which will have certain outward forms of Christianity, but in fact will be an instrument of the rule of Antichrist. The book has been influential in many Orthodox countries, including Russia and Greece where Seraphim Rose is widely read.

The book left a great impression on me, and over the following years I became aware of how rapidly the things described by Father Seraphim were not only coming to fruition, but were in fact going beyond anything he had described. The extent to which occultism has penetrated mainstream culture in Western Europe and North America led me to consider writing something that would follow up on the themes he wrote about, and examine just how far the satanic agenda has advanced.

In 2016 I began researching the topics he dealt with, exploring how our society is being shaped by occult forces. But as I read, I began to recognise that there is a more disturbing side to what is happening that Father Seraphim had not written about. I found that powerful institutions and international corporations are working to an evil agenda, and that this agenda is intrinsically hostile to the authentic Church.

As Christians we understand that human history has a spiritual dimension which is ignored by humanistic historians. We know that the whole of time is working according to God's plan of salvation, and that to apply this perspective to world events is to gain a true understanding of what is happening. This book is an attempt to do just this, and so reveal something of the agenda that is the real motivation and driving force behind what is presented to us as just the way the world is.

Watching old footage of news coverage of the assassination of President Kennedy it becomes clear how quickly people were aware that the official narrative did not match the facts. Within days of the event a number of journalists were publicly stating that a conspiracy was at work. In the following decades, many writers have tried to publicise different conspiracies, but with no widespread interest from the mainstream media (MSM). Since the emergence of the internet, information has been far more available to the public, and many more people have begun to recognise deliberate plans behind many terrible events. As a reaction the MSM frequently uses the phrase "conspiracy theory" to dismiss the claims: in fact many people today who watch television will automatically think of the word "theory" when they hear "conspiracy". This manipulation has led to an instant dismissal of many concerns about the activities of elite organisations and powerful corporations; it is like pressing a red button marked "tin foil hat". Part of this is due to the fact that most people find it difficult to accept that their own government could be part of something so terrible; it would require a complete change in world view for many. This would be painful, frightening and possibly too threatening to risk, and the MSM is only too happy to provide enough distractions to help us stop thinking about such matters.

I am fully aware that there are readers who will object to some of the things I have written. I also understand that there will be groups who dismiss or attack both me and this book: these are inevitable reactions. But my hope is that while there is time, I can add my voice to those who are naming evil for what it is, in the face of a satanic kingdom that is armed with every weapon the world can provide. As I began to recognise the same forces behind so many of the events and situations around the world, I realised that more than anywhere else, the true nature of what is happening is revealed in war; and so this is where the book begins. The book then looks at some of the evidence of what is happening around us, before pointing to where it is leading. The second half of the book is concerned with the means by which the satanic kingdom is attacking and manipulating our thinking. The final chapter then reflects on some of the prophetic voices that have emerged from within the Church and the clear warnings they have given us about what is to come, and how we should prepare ourselves.

Chapter 1 ~ War

Libya is in chaos. Various jihadist groups, including Islamic State, are bringing real terror to civilians while two rival governments struggle as much with each other to gain control as with the terrorists. Militias continue to operate outside of government direction and there is little hope of any functioning judiciary being established soon. For those Libyans who remain, life consists of roadblocks, power cuts, the sound of gunfire and fear. To read of this appalling state of affairs is to wonder whether the western military attacks on Libya were worth it. But this question assumes that there was a stated aim that was or was not achieved, or that our government participated in a war on Libya because of some democratic or just motive that has been explained to us and agreed upon. But the deeper we look into the case of Libya, the clearer it becomes that what we have been told is not true. But it gets worse, because as we examine the facts, we discover that not only politicians but our newspapers, the BBC, the United Nations, in fact almost every agency that governs or keeps us informed, is in on the lie.

Let us begin with the basic question: why did we bomb Libya? For many people the immediate response will be some formulation of the idea that General Gaddafi was an evil dictator, and during what the media called the Arab Spring the people of Libya rose up and needed our support to establish freedom in their country. It is a simplistic, almost infantile summary, but it sums up what the journalists were telling us. But this reduction of reality to uncomplicated ideas is dangerous. It would be equally misleading to paint Gaddafi as a good man, he clearly was not. The accounts of human rights abuses paint a picture of an oppressive and dictatorial leader. But the reality of life under Gaddafi was complicated, and unless we look at the full picture we fail to see how we are led by our media to accept our governments' actions and explanations with too little scrutiny.

In 1967 Colonel Gaddafi took control of one of the poorest nations in Africa. Before he was killed, Libya's population had a higher life expectancy than any other Africans and also enjoyed the highest GDP on the continent. In fact, there were less Libyans living under the poverty line than in some Western European countries, and on top of this the nationalised oil guaranteed free education and health care to all, male and female: he raised literacy rates from twenty percent to eighty-three percent. Women had the freedom to dress as they wanted and study at the universities which, of course, are now shut down. More than half of Libya's higher education students under Gaddafi were women, and they were given the right to hold jobs, own property, seek divorce, and claim an equal income to men due to the equal work law that he passed within a year of being in office. Many of the Islamic groups fighting for control of Libya today are utterly opposed to these opportunities for women.

These policies were supported by a public declaration of his personal philosophies that underpinned a society that promoted social justice. In Gaddafi's Libya having a home was considered a human right, but furthermore he stated that home ownership itself was a necessary element to human freedom, and promised that his parents, who were living in a tent, would not be properly housed until he had done so for all other Libyans. He pronounced every man's right to food, clothing and transport as sacred and recognised society at large as having no authority to interfere with the individual's personal choices. Gaddafi recognised state control of education as a dangerous means of influence and insisted that no one be forced to follow a particular curriculum or even study set subjects: he described such rules as manipulation and coercion. Libya had a state bank which rejected usury and so Libyan citizens could take out loans without having to pay interest.

The picture becomes increasingly complicated when we consider Gaddafi's standing amongst other African nations. His plan was to use a portion of Libya's oil profits to help with the reconstruction of Africa and so enable food self-sufficiency. Gaddafi launched Africa's first communications satellite which freed many millions of Africans from paying the high fees demanded by European corporations and today there are many parts of Africa which have more developed communications networks than the United Kingdom. Gaddafi carried out the world's largest irrigation project, called the Great Manmade River Project, which made water available to areas of previously desert land.

Gaddafi was praised by Nelson Mandela as one of the world's greatest freedom fighters and the South African president recognised the downfall of his country's apartheid system as owing much to Gaddafi's support. It is notable that this support came at a time when the U.K. government under Margaret Thatcher was actively supporting the white South African regime. For centuries before western involvement in slavery there had been a long history of Arabs enslaving Africans, and Gaddafi is the only Arab leader to have made a formal apology for his nation's part in it. For many commentators it was his desire for a strong, united Africa that put him at odds with western powers such as the United States. For example, in August 2011 President Obama confiscated thirty billion dollars from Libya's central bank, which had been earmarked by Gaddafi for the establishment of an African central bank: something which would have challenged the authority of the western banks and so limited western influence in African affairs. Furthermore he had been deliberately investing in projects that reduced the dependency of African nations on the West, with the ultimate goal of establishing African economic independence. Western governments objected to his support of national liberation organisations that were perceived to be in opposition to western control, all of which made Gaddafi a rival to U.S. influence in Africa just at the time when Chinese corporations were extending their own government's influence by increasing investment in African projects.

But then the western news networks related the narrative of the Arab Spring, familiar and reliable newsreaders told us of how freedom was being grasped by the oppressed. Within a week (February 25th) of protests in Libya starting, Nicolas Sarkozy in Paris was announcing on television that "Gaddafi must go". Three days later U.K. Prime Minister David Cameron announced that he was working to establish a no-fly zone (often the first step in western military action) over Libya: all of this without any kind of diplomatic attempts to reach the Gaddafi government. A month later it was reported in the New York Times that CIA operatives had "for some weeks" been active in Libya. Let us just pause for a moment and register the timeline. This statement was made in the New York Times on 30th March, which meant they had been operating in Libya since at least the middle of

February which is when the first protests had begun. It was later confirmed that the CIA had been supported in Libya by MI6 and British Special Forces and that president Obama had signed an agreement for the CIA to arm and support the rebels. Using the Arab Spring as cover, the U.S.A. had begun military operations in Libya while Obama publicly declared the intention was regime change.

We might wonder how a free and independent press covered these events. David Cameron had argued that a no-fly zone was necessary because Gaddafi was about to bomb the Libyan people. In the same month (February) the BBC reported that Gaddafi's jets had opened fire on protesters and without question repeated government reports of the threat of genocide. In fact just a few days later, on 1st march even the U.S. Secretary of Defence Robert Gates admitted at a Pentagon press conference that there was no evidence or confirmation that any such attacks by Gaddafi's air force had taken place.

But still the idea that military action must be taken to protect civilians was propagated by the interventionists through the BBC. At the end of March Obama was insisting that military action was preventing a "blood bath" in Benghazi. Later it was discovered that the French air attack described in this way had been on a column of ambulances and other trucks that was not only insufficient to pose any threat to the people of Benghazi, but in fact it was retreating from the city. While the BBC persisted with its theme of an approaching slaughter, Gaddafi, wanting to avoid further violence, had created an escape route for the rebels so that they could escape to Egypt.

The narrative was developed further when the U.S. Ambassador, Susan Rice, informed the UN Security Council that Gaddafi was supplying his troops with Viagra tablets in order that they could carry our mass rapes. Despite her complete lack of evidence to support this lurid claim the story was accepted by the UN and repeated through the media. In fact the claim was utterly false, it was completely rejected by US military intelligence sources and even the UN's Cherif Bassiouni had to admit on 10th June that such stories were, as he called them, "mass hysteria". But by June the media had moved on, recognition of such lies was unimportant, and the momentum of the anti-Gaddafi narrative had become too strong. No one was interested in looking back over their shoulders and admitting how wrong they had been, especially the news broadcasters. When the dust had settled, Amnesty International was to investigate the claims of mass rape by Gaddafi forces, and in an interview with the French newspaper Liberation, admitted that they had found "no cases of rape. Not only have we not met victims, but we have not found anyone who knows of such victims".

But the eventual revelation of the truth didn't matter. So long as public opinion could be sufficiently swung behind the military action while it was taking place, then the news stories were fulfilling their purpose. When it was discovered that NATO had deliberately targeted Libya's state television, killing three civilians, a few journalists were horrified at the deaths of their own, but the story was no longer newsworthy (despite the action being a violation of international law). NATO protected rebels and enabled them to starve the civilians of Tripoli of food, water and fuel during the war, but the media was silent, while accusing Gaddafi of doing exactly the same thing elsewhere. Newspapers such as The Times, The Guardian and The Telegraph repeatedly printed claims that Gaddafi was using African mercenaries to fight his people and yet Human Rights Watch not only found no evidence to support this but did discover many cases where these stories had resulted in the murder of groups of black people in Libya who were suspected of being mercenaries.

Today it is estimated that there are thousands of Libyans displaced within their land and over a million have fled to other countries such as Egypt and Tunisia. Oil production has collapsed to a third of its output and many people complain of being months behind in their wages, driving many disaffected young men into the arms of extremist Islamic groups whose ideologies are flourishing in

Libya. But despite all this, NATO declared its war in Libya "one of the most successful in NATO history". It may appear at first a ridiculous statement: how, we might wonder, could the destruction of a nation state and the resulting carnage and increase in jihadism be considered successful? Of course, it only looks ridiculous when we try to view it all with the understanding of ordinary people. Most of us assume that the desire for justice, truth, safety and so on are the common values that our governments share too. Through such eyes the war in Libya was a catastrophe. The U.S. has spent trillions of dollars fighting wars over the last decade, and as a result it has established military bases in Kuwait, Qatar, Bahrain, as well as Kazakhstan, Uzbekistan, Kenya, South Sudan, Niger, Burkina Faso and many, many others (interestingly Russia has only two military bases outside its borders and yet the BBC repeatedly refers to "Russian aggression"). So who has succeeded? Out of all of this the one group that has benefited more than any other is the U.S. military industrial complex. Not the Libyan people now living in fear, not western populations having terrorist acts visited upon them by vengeful jihadists, but the military elite.

Whichever way we read this story, there are questions that must be asked. Why would different governments be so eager to support military action which has no obvious benefit for their own people or the population of the country being attacked? Why would the news media fail to report the basic facts, let alone hint at the complexity of the war that has prolonged and broadened the suffering of the Libyan people? It may simply be that such action advances the interests of the military and trans-national corporations who also own the media. But as I shall attempt to make clear, I do not believe that greed and corruption are the entire answer. They play their part, but the full picture must be understood from a deeper perspective. Before we look at the groups involved, let us first look a little closer at the arms corporations.

In 1999, the South African president, Thabo Mbeki, signed up for defence deals which would cost his country five billion dollars. In the same year he publicly declared that South Africa did not have the funds necessary to make available antiretroviral medication to the five million of its citizens who had contracted HIV. Harvard University later conducted research which revealed that between the years 2000 and 2005, 330,000 South Africans died of AIDS because they could not afford treatment. As the group Control Arms Campaign has shown, the vast majority of arms sales go to less economically developed countries (what we once called The Third World); South Africa is far from alone in seeing its resources used in this way. While these specific examples are useful in focussing our attention on what is happening, and there are more to come, we must look at the bigger picture if we are really to understand it.

Though the positions change a little year by year, it has become something of a cliché to state that the five countries that are the largest arms dealers also happen to be the five permanent members of the United Nations Security Council: they are U.S.A., Russia, France, U.K. and China. There is some variation in the order, for example the tiny nation of Israel was in fourth position in 2007, having sold over 4.4 billion dollars' worth of arms that year. But out in front is the U.S.A. which repeatedly accounts for over sixty percent of arms trade (Western Europe accounts for over 30%). The amount of money involved is astonishing; the U.S.A. alone spends over seventy billion dollars a year on defence (in 2008, during the Iraq and Afghanistan conflicts, U.S. spending had risen by 83% compared with 2000, which was more than the next 46 states added together). It is estimated that the world spends over a hundred billion dollars a year on small arms alone, and according to Small Arms Survey, there are now over a hundred countries involved in their manufacture. The money involved is extraordinary, but the consequences in human life are worse. The Geneva Declaration on Armed Violence and Development estimates that fatalities due to armed violence account for over half a million deaths per year.

But even in the face of such astronomical figures we might still wonder if all of this is simply the necessary price to maintain freedom, justice, democracy and safety. After all, we might suggest our governments are part of the international community, they are working for the good of mankind. Certainly there are steps taken to present themselves in this way. Delegates from the UN member states met in New York in 2011 to agree on an arms trade treaty (ATT) in order, we were told, to regulate arms trade and ensure our common values were being respected and protected. In his research, Andrew Feinstein discovered that despite the ATT, up to 40% of economic corruption in the world is directly linked to the arms trade. For example he points out that as a result of the wars in Iraq and Afghanistan, U.S. arms manufacturers and dealers made billions of dollars in profit and operated what he described as a "revolving door" policy with the U.S. government: as officials left their posts they would be employed by the defence companies only to return to government posts later.

The problem goes deeper, however, as the Security Council members ensured that the ATT provides legally binding safeguards for governments to spend as much of their budget on defence as they see fit, and since 1947 the World Trade Organisation has similarly excluded arms trade from all agreements on trade tariffs. International trade is thus arranged so that tyrannical despots are assured by the UN and WTO that there can be no imposition of limits to their spending of their nations' money on the very weapons being sold by the members of the Security Council. In every international trade agreement a clause is inserted which guarantees exemption of any policy deemed vital for national security, a loophole that permits unlimited military spending). This approach is reflected in governments' own laws with regard to arms deals. Western states continue to demand and protect their right to trade in arms with countries which use these weapons on their own citizens and it is extremely rare for arms dealers to face prosecution over their refusal to follow even the relaxed rules that do govern their trade.

To demonstrate that this is more than rhetoric, let us consider the conflict in the Yemen (still ongoing at the time of writing). Countries such as the Netherlands, Sweden and Switzerland have acknowledged that the ATT outlaws sales of arms to states known to be using those weapons on civilians, and so have refused to sell to Saudi Arabia which has been proven to be bombing civilians. The U.K., France and the U.S. have continued to sell small and heavy weapons to the Saudis, the U.K. going so far as to chide those who criticise their conduct as being likely to discourage other nations from signing up to the ATT if they think they will be criticised in this way. The U.K.

has a long history of this kind of action. In the 1970s it was selling Chieftain Tanks to the Iranian Shah who was known to be using them against student protestors.

The arms trade lacks transparency like no other form of trade. It is a murky world where deals are made without public scrutiny. It is not surprising then that it should become so corrupt. In 2010 the U.K. company BAE (the second largest arms manufacturer in the world) was fined four hundred million dollars for making bribes to secure deals in Eastern Europe. BAE was found to be making payments of millions of dollars into Swiss bank accounts as well as using false accounting and making misleading statements. It is worth noting that an investigation by the Serious Fraud Office in 2006 was cancelled when Saudi officials became concerned that their own corruption might be uncovered.

The big picture involves the geopolical interests of governments; arms deals are a means of promoting influence and control. Talk at inter-government level is often focussed on control of nuclear weapons, and these are the stories that the media promotes. But the vast sales of conventional weapons go largely unreported, and so the reality is never disclosed. U.S.A., France and U.K. often make more profit in sales of arms to developing countries than they give in aid. And the recipients of this aid are also carefully selected: for example

India received aid from the U.K. while continuing to be the largest customer for the arms trade in the world.

As the so-called economic crisis brought policies of austerity to bear on various populations, markets for arms trade were also hit. The arms manufacturers were, like any other company, forced to seek out new markets, and nothing is better for their business than war or the fear of war. J.W. Smith (in his book The World's Wasted Wealth) demonstrates that both states and arms companies have been involved in encouraging warlike policies amongst developing nations by creating a sense of threat from other states and terrorists. False reports have been identified coming from the arms traders which exaggerate the military capacity of other nations and so increase the sales of their goods. At the same time subsidies are made available by governments to provide tax breaks for military development: we the tax payers are subsidising the arms industry.

Since the events of 9/11 the U.S. government has enabled its arms manufactures to branch out into previously closed markets. George W. Bush revised the list of countries to which arms could be sold under the pretext that any state fighting in America's war on terror could be sold or even given weapons. This has led to arms deals being made with states previously prohibited from such deals because of their human rights records. Bush was even able to pass a three hundred million funding allocation to support countries' classified activities in this struggle: in other words no account had to be given for where or to whom this money was sent. This kind of aid and support has enabled the U.S. government to extend its influence around the world, often supporting oppressive regimes: some argue that this has partly led to the development of extremist political and religious groups who see the U.S. as propping up unjust dictatorships. The World Policy Institute found that the U.S. is "routinely funnelling military aid and arms to undemocratic nations" and of the twenty-five countries in the developing world which have been given aid in the form of arms, thirteen of them have been classed as undemocratic even by the U.S. State department.

A picture emerges of an arms trade that is not simply a means of producing wealth or security, but is used to shape national and foreign policy and gives strategic influence over many regions of the world. For example, when the U.S. agreed to sell eighty F16s to the United Arab Emirates (at a price of approximately fifteen billion dollars) it was also given permission to build military bases there, giving the U.S. a powerful means of controlling the Persian Gulf. Bases have been built in Turkey following other arms deals despite Turkey's long and recent history of human rights violations. The same arms dealers are selling their weapons to both

Pakistan and India, even giving away many of their highest level military developments requiring that their own research be expanded further on the grounds that other states now have such sophisticated weaponry.

Politicians often describe their trips to foreign states as humanitarian or fact finding, but in reality they are making deals for the arms companies. On a visit to India (in 2002) Tony Blair talked to the press about the effects of earthquakes and a desire to end conflict between Pakistan and India: later it was discovered that over half his time in the country was spent persuading the Indian government to buy sixty-six Hawk jets at a cost of one point four billion dollars. Our politicians present their purpose and role as serving us and seeking justice, but in reality are working for these enormous arms manufacturers.

In his farewell address, U.S. President Eisenhower warned his people that "we must guard against the acquisition of unwarranted influence, whether sought or unsought, by the military, industrial complex. The potential for the disastrous rise of misplaced power exists and will persist." In fact, as we can see, that misplaced power has grown immeasurably. But those who wield it control far more than the sale and use of weapons. Once we begin to see the scale of corruption and deceit that surrounds the arms trade and the decisions taken that lead us to war, it is only wise to wonder who benefits from such conditions, and therefore, who is promoting this reality? Similarly we might continue to ask why our media isn't alerting us to what is going on and what underlying goal is being pursued.

Chapter 2 ~ The United Nations

On the 25th April, 1945, delegates from fifty nations met in San Francisco for a conference they called the United Nations Conference on International Organisation. After nine weeks of intense negotiations, a ten thousand word Charter was approved and passed by every delegate present. Just four months later, on 24th October the United Nations was officially born as representatives signed off on the new venture. The vision driving all this was summed up as "humanity under one roof" and other, similarly attractive slogans that decent minded people could hardly oppose. The new collective, global conscience of this organisation was expressed in 1948 as the Universal Declaration of Human rights which again used the kind of language that would make anyone opposing it seem like a bigot or deeply uncaring. Since its creation the UN has been promoted as the world organisation that can be called upon when there are natural disasters or when evil governments are seen to use excessive force on their people. This is the popular view presented on reliable sources such as the BBC, with little scrutiny given to the enormous groups of agencies through which the UN has expanded its involvement in almost every aspect of so many people's lives. But as will be demonstrated here, the reality is very different; the UN is founded on New Age principles promoted by the likes of Alice Bailey (much more about her later), the founder of the Lucifer Trust. First we will consider the philosophy behind the UN which is directly opposed to Christian teaching, and which will ultimately have to come into direct conflict with those who maintain Orthodox Christianity. Already we have hints of this conflict; in November 2016 the EU officially listed the Russian Orthodox Church as one of the opponents of European, liberal culture (on a list that included a number of extreme political and religious groups). Western liberals are already firing warning shots across the bows of the Church.

The media presents the UN solely as a secular organisation, but in order to grasp its purpose and aims we must examine its religious principles. Its members promote it as the answer to man's longing for peace in the world, the body which will create social order, and opponents of which are denounced as evil heretics. The fact is, the whole UN agenda is driven by the principles of the Enlightenment, particularly in terms of its vision of man. The UN has two guiding doctrines that we will examine in detail: that is that mankind can be saved through the application of law, and that absolute belief in moral or eternal truths are opposed to this law.

The UN maintains that peace can be established between nations by the imposition of international laws (world laws). The Charter itself establishes the UN's role as being to establish and maintain universal peace. To this end the UN seeks the goal of collective security by means of universal enforceable disarmament. In other words, sovereign nations must give up their ability to determine and protect their nation's values and way of life for the good of the whole human race. To achieve this the original UN Charter identifies the goal of an international society, one which recognises all humanity living as a single moral entity.

Let us look more closely at the first of these guiding principles, that universal peace can only be achieved through international law. If we recognise the UN's ultimate goal as being equivalent to the Christian concept of salvation, we begin to get a better understanding: for each is the purpose and final prize for which the UN and the Church struggles. The principle is alive and well in both Judaism and social gospel Protestantism, the idea that the law can save us. This sits in direct opposition to Orthodoxy which recognises that the law can only condemn: Christ alone is the means of our salvation. Similarly, the law can never save society from war since the cause of war is not a lack of adherence to law, but the fallen nature of man. However determined we may be to impose law, it can never establish peace in the world, only the work of the Holy Spirit in each of us can overcome conflict. The UN in its founding Charter declares itself the means by which mankind will be saved from the scourge of war, it thus seeks to save mankind through the efforts of man himself. The Enlightenment vision of man's rational capacity is established as the ultimate means of fulfilling our ideals.

The second driving principle develops from the first: that the rule of law is to be recognised as the ultimate morality. We only have to look back at the U.S.S.R. which itself was ruled by idealistic law to see that law itself is dependent on the kind of body or state which is making those laws. The countless thousands of Christian martyrs are witness to how demonic such law can be when faith in God is considered alien to that law. The rule of international law requires a universal agreement as to what is just, and since Christian values cannot be of this world, followers of Christ inevitably come into conflict with secular world governance. But we should feel alarmed at this, as President Wilson said to Congress, "The right is more precious than peace."

The essential difference between the international law of the UN and the values of Christianity is that secular bodies deny any possibility of natural law that is God given; therefore law is to be created by man according to man's desires or values. There can be no common ground between the law of God written in men's hearts and the aspirations of fallen man seeking to impose his will on the world. This is where Christians face a dangerous trap. In order to overcome this difference, the UN seeks to satisfy the common principles of not just different Christian groups, but all religions. The UN works to promote multi-faith agreement on core values found in very different belief systems, and so these common values are then identified as the important and central teachings that must be upheld, while other "peripheral" teachings can easily be abandoned. The consequence is that those religious groups which hold firm to their sacred doctrines are portrayed as rejecting the core values of brotherhood, union and love. As we shall see later, the ecumenical movement is a deliberate attempt to strip Orthodoxy of its unique message and portray it as evil.

This absence of true consensus leads us to recognise the true shared value that lies at the heart of the UN's vision of world law. If nations which maintain systems of belief and ethics which are directly opposed to one another, how is international law to incorporate them into its new social system? The question is really where do the law makers find common ground, what is the shared value on which these laws can be based? Though China does not share many western values, it must play its part in the UN because it is a powerful nation: international law cannot function if powerful players do not participate in the game. The true nature of international law rests, not on shared values, but on power. The UN is not a body concerned with morality or truth, but the use of power.

The underlying problem with the UN is that in order to function it must present itself as humanistic. Humanism reflects the Enlightenment doctrine of man's capacity to organise the world in order to satisfy man's needs, and the Charter makes it clear that all people must accept and live in obedience to the UN's principles. Even those nations which do not sign up to the Charter will be forced to act in accordance with its principles. For example, the Declaration of Human Rights insists that there be equivalence, equality for all faiths and beliefs within a nation. But since almost every nation has its own religious or ethnic orientation which is expressed in laws and culture, the UN will obliterate such differences in order to cultivate a universal mode of being human. This is the consequence of its humanism, it identifies the distinctiveness of faith and morality as being divisive, the goodness of man is undermined by his allegiance to a particular set of doctrines or even a particular national identity.

A further difficulty for Christians is the question of where the UN laws come from. Since the members of the UN have no binding customs or historical union, and since all notions of divinely revealed law are rejected, the laws it produces will inevitably be opposed by some groups around the world. The kind of law imposed by the UN is not a shared set of values but a demand for particular types of behaviour, and since its humanism is in conflict with religious values it must suppress or eradicate those beliefs. Even during the Second World War the Federal Council of Churches (consisting of Jews, Protestants and Roman Catholics) proposed a new world order that would bind men through a common inner morality. It is interesting to note that the World Council of Churches has been an ardent supporter of the UN and as far back as 1963 Pope John XXIII, in his encyclical Pacem in Terris was calling for a worldwide community free of any Christian belief. The present Pope, Francis, has made similar calls for a humanistic vision of man and has stated that the world's peace is dependent on the UN. This humanism identifies our problems as the conflict between men, not man's turning away from God.

The underlying philosophy of the UN is presented in humanistic terms, and the language of its publications is charged with ideas that are aimed at inspiring us to accept its solutions for the world. The outward appearance of an atheistic humanism satisfies an increasingly Godless West, but in fact, its agenda has been directed by occultists from its very creation. Before looking at some examples of what the UN is doing, let us consider who is guiding it and from where these basic principles come.

Alice Bailey was one of the founders of what is today referred to as the New Age Movement. She founded an organisation called the Lucifer Trust which has further spread its influence through the creation of other groups: the present headquarters of the UN is located on the very site where she established the Lucifer Trust. Before looking at the principles she developed which will strike you as an unnerving blueprint of what we see happening around us, and how her writings have influenced the UN, let us first identify who she is.

Alice Bailey was born Alice Latrobe Bateman in 1880 and died in 1949; she lived long enough to see the UN come into existence. She was raised in a wealthy British setting and becoming aware of the poverty in Victorian England she came to blame the source of social inequalities on what she called the "theology of the past", principally traditional Christianity. She admitted in her autobiography to having made three attempts at suicide between the ages of five and fifteen because she considered life not worth living. At twenty-two she married Walter Evans, an Episcopalian minister who was abusive and beat her. When she finally left him, in 1915, after he had thrown her down a flight of stairs, she felt she had separated herself not only from this abusive man but also Christianity.

It was in the same year that she separated from her husband that she was introduced to the Theosophical Society, a group of self-proclaimed occultists concerned not just with esoteric matters but the shape and guidance of society. She quickly rose through the organisations ranks and became editor of the society's magazine. In her autobiography she tells how, in 1919 and for the next thirty years she was visited by an unseen spirit which convinced her to record his teachings which became the basis for twenty-eight books. Incidentally, in 1919 the man she was to later marry and take her name, Foster Bailey, a thirty-second degree Freemason, became National Secretary of the Theosophical Society. Bailey claimed, and no doubt believed, that the voices speaking to her were of Tibetan masters, and this caused her to fall out with the society, although she continued to promote many of its ideas.

One of her key ideas was the evolution of human consciousness; something that she believed transcends all religions. In fact she argued that the true cause of human division is the spirit of separateness found in religions like Christianity which she claimed cut people off from the rest of humanity. Her teaching was a principle of ecumenism, that all religions have an essential oneness that they share beyond their outward doctrines. But most important was her ten-point plan which she believed was necessary to bring about a single world order. While these other details about her life and beliefs give us a useful understanding of where she was coming from, it is these ten points that we must pay close attention to if we are to understand what is happening in our world today.

Bailey's first point was to have God and prayer to Him removed from all schools. This has happened in the U.S.A. and is certainly close to being accomplished in most UK state schools. She declared that the aim of this was to "ensure that children are freed from the bondage of Christian culture." The purpose here is to make faith in God a secondary matter, not something worthy of attention in a place of learning.

Her second point was to reduce parental authority over children. The aim here, she admitted, is to "break the communication between parent and child." Bailey recognised that the Christian faith is primarily passed from one generation to the next through the family, and that to end the former the latter must be attacked. It is interesting to note that successive UK governments are desperate to promote greater child care, and even provide families with financial help to break the bond between mother and child, rather than use the financial resources available to increase a father's pay so that a mother is not forced to abandon her children to strangers.

Bailey's third point was the necessity to destroy the traditional Christian family structure. She believed the traditional forms of family were oppressive but also formed the foundation for nations. She believed that by "liberating" people from families we will also see the destruction of nations. In order to achieve this goal Bailey identified the need to promote sexual promiscuity as a norm through the media. A short examination of television and different kinds of advertising will quickly confirm how far this point has been embraced.

The fourth of Bailey's points was to make abortion available to all. She argued that abortion clinics should be built and health clinics established in schools to advise children about how to access these services. Few schools in the UK publicise the fact that they make the "morning after pill" freely available to students without parental involvement. Bailey understood that this was necessary if young people were to be encouraged to live promiscuous life styles. Once more she believed that Christian attitudes to abortion were an infringement on people's rights and oppressive.

Point five was free people from the concept of marriage as a commitment for life. To this end Bailey promoted easy and quick divorces which she knew would help to undermines the value and meaning of marriage.

Bailey's sixth point was the establishment of homosexuality as an alternative lifestyle. Once more rejecting Christian morality as oppressive she said that people should be "free" to have sex with whoever they wish, so long as it is consensual. She believed that this extended to incestuous and adulterous relationships. She described how this could only be achieved if it was done under the language of tolerance and acceptance with an eventual goal of destroying gender distinction. Already in 2017 we hear liberal voices insisting that gender is no longer to be considered a matter of biology, but a matter of choice.

The seventh point in Bailey's plan was the debasement of art. She described the arts as a means of changing culture and understood that they could be used to desensitise people and so destroy the sense of what is unacceptable in society. Through corruption of the imagination, people are thus freed from the outmoded concepts that she argued imprisoned people's minds, and she also understood that traditional art can lead people to a sense of the spiritual.

Bailey's eighth point was to alter people's consciousness through the various forms of media. She wanted the normalisation of hedonism that would then overcome the old social norms and so enable the establishment of new ways of living and being. The producers of the T.V. series "Will And Grace" claimed that their portrayal of gay characters had a greater influence on the U.S. population's acceptance of homosexuality than any educational or political effort.

The ninth point was to establish a worldwide interfaith movement. Through this Bailey believed it was possible to break down the perception of Christianity as being something unique or special. Once more the language of tolerance would enable all religions to be given equal standing, particularly in the minds of children, creating the foundations of a single world religion. Evidence for how this is being implemented can be seen in the statement of the Satanic Temple in Oklahoma. In defending their erection of a seven foot tall statue of Satan immediately next to an older statue in the city depicting the Ten Commandments (something the city's officials considered a reasonable thing to do) the group stated: "Our purpose is not to denigrate any religion or faith, which would be repugnant to our educational purposes, but instead to learn and experience the history of different cultural practices."

In his January 2017 Christmas address to the nation, President Putin identified one of the failings of the West as being a pluralism that permits Satanism to be given equal standing to Christianity because of a political correctness that demands all beliefs to be treated with equal validity; Bailey's intention entirely.

Her final point was that these nine points should not only be made law by governments but that they should be approved by Christian bodies. She said that the goal was to get churches to change their doctrines but that this could only be achieved through these nine points. Throughout her programme the enemy is never religion per se, it is not extremist groups who slaughter the innocent: the enemy is Christianity.

It is disturbing to reflect on how far the West has travelled along Bailey's road to a new world order. There is nothing in her points that we cannot see in the society around us, Bailey's strategy has been and is being implemented in ways that go unobserved by most people. It is interesting to note that, as yet, these ideas are firmly rooted in the West but not in places like Asia, Africa and South America. When the primates of the Anglican Church gather in England, we see the media delighting in how whoever is Archbishop of Canterbury of the day struggling to present western ideas to the African bishops. Primarily on issues of sexuality, the Africans are repeatedly portrayed as bigoted men who have been left behind, they are an embarrassment to the western clergy so keen to embrace the new world view and present the modern (and acceptable to the world) face of Anglicanism.

But while we can so clearly see how Bailey has provided a blueprint for how western culture has developed since 1945, let us also confirm how it is not only her ideas which are at the heart of the UN, but see the extent to which her organisations have direct influence at the meetings of the UN delegates.

The Lucifer Publishing Company was set up by Bailey in 1920, but because the name revealed a little much, it was changed in 1922 to the Lucis Trust. Today the Lucis Trust has consultative status at the United Nations. This position gives its representatives a seat on the weekly sessions, providing direct influence on the members of the UN and the direction the UN moves. But the Lucis Trust does not simply have influence through its official position at the UN, its trustees have included John Rockefeller, Thomas Watson (former US ambassador), Henry Kissinger and various members of the US Council On Foreign Relations. The Windsor bank has in the past acknowledged itself as a contributor to the Lucis Trust (but the details have now been removed from its website). The former Assistant Secretary General of the UN (and winner of a UNESCO Prize for Peace Education) Robert Muller, established schools which he has openly stated are rooted in the teachings of Alice Bailey. This is typical of the Lucis Trust which recognises the importance of targeting children for the spread of its ideas: they are well aware of the importance of playing the long game.

The World Goodwill organisation, includes signatories such as Helmut Schmidt (the then Chancellor of West Germany), Malcom Fraser (former Prime Minster of Australia), Shimon Peres and Jimmy Carter. It was founded in 1932 by members of the Lucis Trust and today has NGO status at the UN. Its goals are openly occult, its purpose is to use links with spiritual beings in order to guide politics towards a single world government. The World Goodwill has links with the World Health Organisation, the Teilhardt Centre and even the World Wildlife Fund. World Goodwill acknowledges the support of UNICEF, Ted Turner (founder of CNN), the US Mission of the UN and Amnesty International. Like the Lucis Trust, World Goodwill also has consultative status at the UN. Its promotional material declares that it is working for the "spiritual evolution of humanity", so that, as Alice Bailey writes, "when the Great One appears, he will take the mystery religions preserved by Freemasonry and make them public." Other bodies created by members of the Lucis Trust include the Findhorn Foundation, The Temple of Understanding (which also has NGO status at the UN) and the Global Forum of Spiritual and Parliamentary Leaders which met in 1988, was attended by the Dalai Lama, the Archbishop of Canterbury, Carl Sagan and various government representatives: one of its conclusions was that the world's population must be reduced.

The UN has a meditation room which is maintained by the Lucis Trust. It contains a four foot tall black stone, one of the largest lumps of magnetite that has ever been discovered. The occultists believe that by meditating before a giant magnet they are able to control certain energies, and for this purpose the stone is grounded into the bed-rock beneath the room. One former Secretary General of the UN, Dag Hammarskjold (second Secretary General of the UN), described this stone as "the symbol of the god of all". It had been at his insistence that the meditation room be built according to its particular dimensions, that is a pyramid without its capstone: he believed that the "spiritual" nature of existence should be at the centre of everything the UN worked for. In his self-penned notes to the meditation room Hammarskjold explained that the empty altar is dedicated to "the God whom man worships under many names and in many forms". This is the basis of the single world religion which anticipates the coming of a "Christ" not in a Christian understanding, but the one who will come to satisfy and fulfil all religions. This terminology is very common in the writings of both Bailey and Teilhard and is echoed in the words of former UN Assistant Secretary General who stated: "We must move as quickly as possible to a one-world government; a one-world religion; under a one-world leader." On the wall of this meditation room hangs a huge mural full of geometric shapes and esoteric symbols including twenty-seven triangles and the al-seeing eye. At its centre is an image of the phoenix rising, not from fire or ashes, but from its shed skin like a serpent. These kinds of details would strike most right-minded people as bizarre, almost unbelievable, it is all so far removed from how ordinary people live: and yet the UN meets to determine the plan for our lives in the midst of what is clearly evil. Let us finally consider just a few of the programmes the UN is working to achieve and the reality behind them.

The UN Agenda 2030 was adopted at the 70th annual UN General Assembly, and is a plan to provide health care for the whole world. Presented in this form it seems a decent, altruistic plan. However, the programme includes the enforced acceptance by nations of what is called sexual and reproductive healthcare: this simply means abortion on demand and contraception must be made available regardless of the religion or culture of a particular country. Already we see the receiving of UN aid being linked to the requirement of accepting these programmes. Agenda 2030 also aims to have every child in the world vaccinated by 2030. Children are identified in the programme as key players, just as Alice Bailey said they must be, the language used in Agenda 2030 describes them as "agents for change". But the programme goes beyond provision of medical care, it aims to control education so that all children are educated concerning what it calls diversity, citizenship and sustainable development (again, a coded reference to population control). The focus is very much on indoctrination of children, teaching them the new values and beliefs that the UN recognises as needed to meet its goals. Agenda 2030 was accepted unanimously and Pope Francis described it as "an important sign of hope".

Another programme few of us have heard of is the UN's New Urban Agenda which was agreed in 2016. This programme aims to determine how cities are organised, with a particular emphasis on environmental sustainability. The use of so-called "green" terminology is a means of promoting greater control by the UN over what sovereign nations are permitted to do. The pattern was established decades ago, when Agenda 21 was passed, and George Bush senior made his infamous comments about establishing a "new world order". Agenda 21 was a major step in the UN's programme of using the threat of a climate change crisis to convince the middle and working classes that they must accept lower wages, population reduction, abortion and a general lowering of their standard of living. Dissenting voices are immediately branded as "deniers" by the likes of the BBC. Praising the UN's health programmes Bill Gates stated:

The world today has 6.8 billion people. That's heading up to about nine billion. Now if we do a really great job on new vaccines, health care and reproductive health services, we could lower that by perhaps ten or fifteen percent.

How revealing that a man applauded in the media for the humanitarian use of part of his vast fortune in making vaccines available sees the purpose of this venture as reducing the number of human beings on earth, not simply saving lives. We shall consider this topic further in a later chapter.

UN involvement with various crises in the world does not have a good record. Besides their disregard of certain ethnic groups, it has long been known that when the blue helmeted peacekeeping troops of the UN roll in, prostitution and drug sales sky rocket. The UN is portrayed as one thing in the media, but as we have seen, in reality is something very different. An organisation so heavily influenced by Satanists is simply not working for good no matter how benevolent they may present themselves as being. But as we reflect on the cultural and social changes that have happened around us, and we see that they have followed exactly what Alice Bailey prescribed, we understand that none of it has come about by accident, or through the natural processes by which societies are said to "evolve": those who control the spiritual agenda of the UN are Satanic. Later we will consider how these changes have been made possible and by what means those seeking to deliver Bailey's vision are working to achieve their aims. The themes touched on so far, one world government, education, sexuality, the media and so on, will all be considered in greater detail. But first let us look beyond the UN and identify other powerful groups that control how our world is being shaped, and the beliefs that dominate their agenda.

Chapter 3 ~ Powerful Elites

The vision of the western world presented to us through the mainstream media is of nations governed by leaders who are accountable to their electorate, and that through the ballot box people have the power to reject political parties when dissatisfied with their performance. All of this rests on the idea that the people know what their governments are doing, that there is sufficient transparency (and honesty amongst politicians and journalists) to reveal what kinds of decisions are being made, and on the public's ability to be able to decide whether those in control are acting on their behalf. We hear political parties setting out their manifestos before elections, we assume that this will be the course followed if the party wins, and above all we are led to assume that when the politicians assure us that they are concerned with our best interests, we should believe them.

But how different it might appear if the mainstream media (MSM) was to reveal that the major decisions about how our nation is governed were being made in secret. But more than this, that decisions were being made about how the whole western world should be organised and also how it should relate to the rest of the world, without any level of accountability or public scrutiny. And then add to this a further ingredient, that the people elected to make these decisions do not do so alone, but sit with bankers, media moguls and heads of international corporations who are able to influence, demand, or offer whatever they like in exchange for ensuring that they get their way without us ever knowing any of the details. How completely different things would appear to the public if the media revealed any of this: but of course the MSM doesn't because it's part of the club.

Since 1954 the Bildeberg Group has been meeting annually, it is a gathering of between one hundred and twenty to a hundred and fifty high powered men, one third of whom are politicians, the rest being from various business interests or specialist fields. The meetings are held under what is called the Chatham House Rule, which means that no one present is permitted to reveal who has participated or make anyone accountable by name for anything they have proposed or offered. This level of secrecy frees the members from any rules, commitments or conventions that might be imposed by rank or office; politicians are not obliged to speak for those who entrusted them with their jobs. No pre-arranged agenda is published, no notes are taken or recorded, and there has never been a policy statement issued by the group.

While this might not strike some as immediately alarming, when we look at who is in attendance we begin to grasp the level of power and influence that is being wielded at the meetings. For example, the 2016 meeting included from the world of finance:

Paul Achleitner, Chairman of the Supervisory Board of Deutsche Bank;

Maria Albuquerque, Former Minister of Finance of Portugal;

Benoit Coere, Member of the Executive Board of the European Central Bank;

John Cyran, CEO of Deutsche Bank and

Michael Noonan, Irish Minister for Finance.

From the world of politics there were:

Kristalina Georgieva, Vice President of the European Commission;

Ursula von der leyen, German Minister of Defence;

Thomas de Maiziere, German Minister of the Interior;

Charles Michel, Belgian Prime Minister;

Mark Rutte, Prime Minister of the Netherlands;

Mehmet Simsek, Turkish Deputy Prime Minister and

George Osborne, the U.K. Chancellor.

Big businesses such as Shell Oil, BP, Google, TalkTalk, Airbus, Volvo, Chrysler and Scottish Power had their CEOs in attendance.

With such a high profile group of people meeting in one place, we might naturally expect heavy media coverage: in fact channels such as the BBC, ITN, Channel 4, CNN et al were indifferent to the event. In fact, until recently, the BBC treated rumours of the group's existence as a conspiracy theory; the label used to dismiss and discredit a wide range of discoveries. This is the established pattern for all of the Bildeberg meetings, but this should not surprise us, key members of the free press make up the guest list. For example, the 2016 meeting included:

Anne Applebaum of the Washington Post;
Richard Engel, Chief Foreign Correspondent of NBC News;
Peggy Noonan of The Wall Street Journal and
Martin Wolf, Chief Economics Commentator of the Financial Times.

Military groups were also represented by key personnel, including Philip Breedlove, the Former Supreme Allied Commander of Europe and other guests have include the heads of MI5, MI6 and the CIA as well as the chief of the International Monetary Fund (IMF).

It would be difficult to imagine a more prestigious and influential guest list, but there is a further core group that attends every meeting whose names remain undisclosed. They gather in various European locations, and without a single TV crew to bother them, they quietly climb into the limousines at the end of their meetings, and return to their roles of influence. Politicians, elected to represent their constituents, make no statements about what has been agreed, and the few independent journalists who have tried to question the departing attendees have been arrested.

The Bildeberg organisation has a website where it reveals that its focus are Geo-politics of energy and commodity prices, migration, technological innovation, debt, Russia, and interestingly, the middle class. Details about how the group aims to have influence over these issues or in what direction it hopes to lead us are not provided. While the members refuse to disclose to us the aims of the group, we need to recognise that what is happening is our finance ministers and powerful bankers are meeting with the heads of huge international corporations to discuss our economic and political systems. We cannot know in any way which of the world's events, crisis or financial slumps is directly linked to their activities, but we can determine other outcomes of their meetings. In 1991 the governor of Arkansas, Bill Clinton, was invited to attend, as was, in 1993, the then shadow Minister Tony Blair. It is certainly possible that the subsequent rise to high office of these men was coincidental to their call to Bildeberg; there is no way for us to know. This is the real difficulty, since it is so shrouded in mystery and lacking in public accountability, we are left guessing, which is disturbing in the context of the level of power attendees of these meetings have. It suggests a top-down pattern of control in the world that is at odds with the perception of democratic systems. The picture takes on an even murkier aspect when we learn that the Bildeberg Group itself was founded by the former SS member Prince Bernard.

In an absence of hard evidence it is too easy to jump to conclusions about the Bildeberg Group, although we might suggest that if the members had nothing to hide they would not cling so desperately to their wall of secrecy. However, we can see concrete evidence of the kinds of activities its members are involved in. For example, member Eric Schmidt, who is estimated to have amassed a personal fortune of over ten billion dollars, is the chairman of Alphabet, Google's parent company. Schmidt has created a company called Groundwork which uses its technology to identify key voters in elections through their activities on social media, and so enable the targeting of political messages and news. It is believed that this helped Obama's 2012 campaign and was also used to support Hillary Clinton (though with less success because she was unable to follow up the information with public appearances in key areas because of her poor health).

Bildeberg raises questions because of its secrecy and the kinds of people who attend. But there are other secret societies that have an equally powerful membership and which have far more sinister aspects. Bohemian Grove is more ancient than Bildeberg and for most ordinary people a description of its activities would seem so bizarre as to be untrue. Powerful heads of state, leaders of business and banking, gather each year to perform occult rituals which include a mock human sacrifice.

Bohemian Grove is a two week, annual gathering of men (exclusively) which has included American presidents such as Reagan, Nixon and the Bushes. Glenn Seaborg, who was awarded the Nobel Prize for chemistry, and who worked on the Manhattan Project (which resulted in the creation of the atomic bomb) described Bohemian Grove as "where all the important people in the United States decide the agenda for our country for the following year". Like Bildeberg, many argue that Bohemian Grove is the necessary platform from which future presidents must launch their hope of office, and certainly in his 1978 memoirs, Richard Nixon acknowledges as much when he says: "If I were to choose the speech that gave me the most pleasure and satisfaction in my political career, it would be my Lakeside Speech at Bohemian Grove in July 1967. Because this speech was off the record, it received no publicity at the time, but in many important ways it marked the first milestone on my road to the presidency."

While the political ramifications of this statement are huge, it is a different aspect of Bohemian Grove that should cause us more concern. Many of those who hold public office, including presidents, will claim to be Christian, often presenting a very devout public persona. But at the Lakeside they participate in what many describe as a pagan ritual, but which I have no hesitation in calling satanic. The ritual is called the "Cremation of Care Ceremony", in which before a forty foot statue of an owl a model of a human body is burned in sacrifice as an offering. The attendees dress in druid-style hooded robes, and the recordings that have been secretly made of the event capture the men shouting and moaning in a chilling fashion. It is the sound of men caught up in something very real, not the beer-fuelled larks they would have the world believe it is. Like Bildeberg, Bohemian Grove is attended by high powered representatives of the mainstream media, and so we should not be surprised that it gains no coverage.

Bildeberg and Bohemian Grove are far from being the only secret gatherings of the elite, others include the Club Of Rome and Skull and Bones (both George Bush and his rival John Kerry were members of Skull and Bones at Yale University, giving the electorate less of a choice than they were led to believe) and when we examine the lists of those in attendance (when possible) we discover that there is a great deal of crossover between the groups: some people even appearing at all of them. The levels of secrecy imposed mean we can only look at the evidence of their actions in the world around us. Here we see the corruption of the arms trade, the apparent recklessness of bankers who bare no responsibility when they cause our economic systems to crash: in fact the consequences of their apparent mismanagement leads to greater rewards for themselves while the majority of people are condemned to live with what is called austerity. And all the time we see a political mood leaning towards greater central control, destruction of sovereign nations, the reduction in political accountability (often called the democratic deficit) and a media hailing the approaching globalised market that will need to be regulated by institutions such as a world bank with an international army. As David Rockefeller said in 1991 (at the German meeting of Bildeberg):

"It would have been impossible for us to develop our plan for the world if we had been subjected to the lights of publicity during those years. But, the world is more sophisticated and prepared to march towards a world government. The supranational sovereignty of an intellectual elite and world bankers is surely preferable to the auto determination practised in past centuries."

These sentiments were echoed by Henry Kissinger at the French meeting of Bildeberg the following year, when he said "individual rights will be willingly relinquished for the guarantee of their well-being granted to them by the world government."

Until the spread of the internet, these kinds of sentiments were expressed quite openly by members of these groups. Today the agenda is more guarded and the language of the UN is of unity, brotherhood and peace. Enough people have become alerted to the programme for a single world governing power that few politicians today will openly admit their intentions. Before we look at how the agenda is being brought to fruition, let us look at some of the other groups and organisations promoting the plan and why they are doing it.

Chapter 4 ~ The European Union

The U.K. referendum decision to leave the European Union has stirred up amongst many people a depth of emotion few political issues could summon. I have no intention of entering the political debate, only to reflect on the facts of how the EU came about and what its goals have been from its inception. Few people who voted in the 2016 referendum had any real understanding of the EU institution because politicians and the media avoided the central issues. We were told the debate was about immigration, or particular laws, or even a vague notion of national sovereignty, while at the same time being given a picture of the EU as an institution that has slowly evolved in response to various economic and political developments. We were presented with superficial caricatures of those who wanted to leave as xenophobic racists while those who wanted to remain were portrayed as wanting to open our borders to all-comers. Emotions were deliberately stirred so as to prevent the majority of people being able to rationally question what was at stake and what the EU is all about. So let us look at the facts, and see where it all started and what its objectives have always been.

The two men who created the plan for the EU were Jean Monet and Arthur Salter. Immediately after the traumatic events of the First World War they conceived of a single European state which would ensure peace in Europe. Their plan from the very beginning was to achieve a single government, but Monet understood that few politicians or peoples would accept this, and so would have to be brought about step by step. The problem, they believed, was that so long as nations elect their own governments, these bodies will be forced to protect the interests of their own people, otherwise democracy would enable their removal from office. Monet and Salter recognised that while the people must outwardly appear to have their own governments, in fact a supranational government would in reality be in power, over which the people would have no democratic control. Their plan would be further supported by the work of an Italian communist, Altiero Spinelli, who in the 1960s worked hard to ensure their final goal of a single government was concealed both from the voting public but also many members of national parliaments.

Monet and Salter had been frustrated while working in the League of Nations (Monet was the League's Deputy-Secretary General) and came to recognise its impotence as being the consequence of each nation having a veto. He wrote in his memoirs that "Goodwill between men, between nations, is not enough. One must also have international laws and institutions". After their work there Monet became a banker in the U.S.A. while Salter developed their theories, publishing a booklet in 1931 called The United States of Europe. Here Salter explained his theories of a federal European state which would be governed by a body made up of international civil servants whose loyalty must be with the European state, not with the individual nations. Only a body without national loyalties, he argued, could be trusted to be above any national governments.

There were already pan-European organisations, but by the 1940s Monet set out to destroy them. For example the Organisation of European Economic Co-operation which administered the funding for the post-war Marshall Plan. Guiding the French government, Monet attacked it because it encouraged national governments to co-operate: this very co-operation stood in the way of the plan for European state. Inter-governmental links would negate the need for any over-arching body, and from the 1940s onwards Monet worked to bring down any such co-operation.

A European crisis over steel production in 1949 enabled Monet to promote a non-governmental body to oversee its production and distribution; concealing his influence, it was known as the Schuman Plan, and was only rejected by Britain because British steel had only just been nationalised by 1950. However, it is interesting to note that while Prime Minister Atlee had recognised the dangers of handing control over such an essential industry to a foreign body, the new Conservative MP for Bexley, in his maiden speech to parliament, declared his support for the handover: his name was Ted Heath. When it came to organising the Plan, Monet managed to have himself appointed chair of the sessions, he was allowed to set the agenda, and though not being a member of the government, he was allowed to represent French interests. The consequence was the establishment of the Council of Ministers, which Monet described in his memoirs as the first real step towards a supranational government. The Shcuman Plan was then agreed at the Treaty of France in 1951.

In his address to the community's members in Luxembourg, he told them that they were meeting as "the first government of Europe". It would be just seven years later that the Council For Europe would meet in Strasbourg, where Robert Schuman was elected president. While Monet avoided too much public exposure at this stage, he began working behind the scenes towards the goal of monetary union. But it is important to understand that for him a single currency was in no way an end in itself, he was well aware of the difficulties this would create for nations with very different economic circumstances, but as he wrote about economic unity: "only with a Financial Common

Market will mutual commitments make it easy to produce the political union which is the goal."

Britain continued to be a problem for Monet because it had longstanding trade agreements with various nations around the world, most notably through the British Commonwealth. Britain continued to favour the concept of inter-governmental co-operation, but this was the enemy of Monet's supranationalism. The Commonwealth was viewed with open hostility by members of the new European Union because it promoted national sovereignty. When Britain finally entered full membership, it was at great expense to many struggling Commonwealth countries that had relied on trade with Britain but were suddenly faced with European tariffs and the destruction of their indigenous industries by the influx of European goods so heavily subsidised that they undercut those locally produced.

Britain's entry into the European Market (as it was still being called – the intention was well hidden) was branded by MP Tony Benn as a "coup d'état by a political class who did not believe in popular sovereignty". Heath's Conservative government managed to win every necessary vote in the House of Commons despite only a slight majority. As the Labour Whip of the day, John Reaper, explained, Labour members were absent from the chamber on a rota so that their absence wouldn't be noticed but which ensured Ted heath's proposals were successful. Of course, the voting public imagining they were being represented by their MPs never heard a word of this.

The variance between public and private opinion is a striking feature of our politicians' involvement with the European project. But so too is the sometimes radical shift in their opinion. For example, in 1983 the newly elected MP for Sedgefield, Tony Blair, assured voters in his election address "We'll negotiate a withdrawal from the EEC, which has drained our natural resources and destroyed jobs." A few years later Blair was pushing for Britain to abandon the pound and enter the Euro zone, an intention only prevented by the then chancellor Gordon Brown.

By the 1980s it was recognised that for the hundreds of millions of people living in Europe, the acceptance of a single government needed the manipulation of people's identity and sense of belonging. The psychology of identity was explored by the commission and it was decided that a common European flag was needed, as well as an anthem, a common passport and driving license and even European teams to compete at international sporting events: this last feature has so far only been established in the world of golf. Towns across Europe would be "twinned" so as to give people a sense of "connection" and schools would have their curriculum altered to reinforce children's understanding of European history and citizenship. It was even hoped that the 9th May would be established as "Europe Day" to celebrate Schuman's success. The idea was that through making the trappings of a national identity associated with a European identity a part of everyday life, the people of Europe would begin to think of themselves differently and so abandon their old national loyalties.

The now infamous Maastricht Treaty was essentially the document that made concrete Spinelli's vision of a true European Union. It included policies which would remove from national governments control over aspects of defence, law, healthcare, consumer rights, education, culture and transport; but symbolically it was when Europeans were officially made citizens of the new order, the European Community. The document was so vast and complex that even after John major's government had signed up to it, they were working for months establishing what it included and what we were committed to. The media focussed on political personalities, about who had been strong or weak, but the public were kept in the dark as to the full impact the legislation would have on their lives. For example, Spanish fishermen, by registering their boats in Britain and purchasing UK fishing licenses, were able to decimate the numbers of fish off British shores and so destroy the UK fishing industry and the communities that depended on it. The BBC chose not to highlight these kinds of realities for fear of the political consequences and potential shift in public opinion.

The selective silence of the U.K. media was demonstrated very clearly when the debate was taking place about Britain's possible entry into the euro zone. Many politicians (such as Kenneth Clark and Michael Heseltine) were given the opportunity by the BBC to present their case for accepting the change in our currency. We were told that it made sense to join a flourishing economy and that we risked being left behind if we stuck with the pound. What these politicians and the BBC failed to tell us was that in 1998 the OBCD figures showed that the British economy had grown beyond that of France to make us the fourth largest in the world, but since it had joined the Common Market the balance of payments between Britain and the EU in trade and contributions to the EU budget was a deficit of a hundred and seventy billion pounds.

As we can see, while political parties and individual politicians shift their position on Europe, the BBC is firmly fixed in its attitude. The goal of a united European, federal state, was clear and intentional from the very beginning of its inception by Monet and the others. Some of us are old enough to recall how those branded as "Euro-sceptics" warned as much for years but were ridiculed as "little Englanders" and anti-Europe itself. But whatever our personal opinion about a federal state, we must ask why the truth was withheld from us. The level of deceit and misinformation from those seeking to establish their European government must raise questions about their moral integrity. In the twenty-first century, with the media focussed on buzzwords like transparency and accountability, we must question the extent to which these words are being used as a kind of slight-of-hand, an assurance of one thing while both the political elite and those at the heart of the media are only too aware of the Orwellian "doublespeak" that is at play. But while this kind of deception may be troubling, it might also be waved away as an example of just what happens in politics. So let us look closer now at the aspects of the EU which suggest something more unsettling.

In 1563 the artist Peter Brueghel painted his interpretation of the Tower Of Babel described in the Book of Genesis in the Old Testament. When designs were being chosen for the European Union's Parliament Building in Strasbourg, it was decided to base the design on Brueghel's image. The similarities are quite startling and clearly no coincidence. In the story from Genesis we are told that "the Lord scattered them abroad from there over the face of the whole earth; and they stopped building." The Strasbourg building has ringed platforms around one side which mimic the look of scaffolding, giving the impression of a work in progress (despite it being completed and in use). For those with access to the internet it is worth taking a moment to compare the painting with the building, the intention is undeniable. The symbolism of many tongues speaking with one voice is a declaration of a new unity, but in fact we see clearly it is a very ancient endeavour. God's intervention was to destroy man's attempts to reach heaven through his own efforts because it was a denial of our need of God. For Christians today this must at least raise questions about the philosophy of those at the heart of the EU.

But this one architectural feature might be dismissed as a coincidence if it was the only example of this spiritual symbolism. Outside the European Council Building in Brussels, however, we find a further sign of the hidden reality (disclosure of secrets in this way is a common feature of occult groups who feel they gain strength from making their plans visible and yet unseen by the majority of people) in the form of a statue of a woman riding a beast. It is very clearly a depiction of what Saint John describes of his vision detailed in the thirteenth chapter of the Book of Revelation: "I stood upon the sand of the sea, and saw a beast rise up out of the sea, having seven heads and ten horns…and all the world wondered at the beast." In John's vision the beast is given power by the dragon to speak blasphemies against God and to make war with the saints.

A further point of interest is that despite the expansion of the EU, no matter how many member states there are the euro coins and notes continue to depict just twelve stars. In many posters these stars are displayed inverted, called inverted pentacles. The occult name for these is The Sigil of the Baphomet and it is one of the official symbols of the world wide Church of Satan. Albert Pike (discussed in detail in the next chapter which is about Freemasonry) demonstrated the clear link between the Goat of Mendes and the inverted star (the two points turned to be at the top of the star represent horns). In Freemasonry it is linked with what they call the Eastern Star which is the name given to the section of Freemasonry established to cater for women, and it is also incorporated into a variety of Masonic imagery on rings and in carvings. The use of the inverted star is a deliberate declaration of intent, and communicates to other participants in occultism the true nature of the organisation. A further point to note is that the U.S. capital, Washington D.C., was planned and built to incorporate a street layout in the form of the pentagram and many monuments and buildings are either directly Masonic symbols or incorporate them in some form. The all-seeing eye was added to the Great Seal of the United States in 1776 and later, in 1935, while Freemason Franklin Roosevelt was president, this image of the Great Seal was added to the one dollar bill and remains there today.

Most of us don't go looking for this kind of symbolism, and our reaction to those who speak about such things can often be to dismiss them as cranks or extreme. And while we cannot give a definitive explanation for the thinking that led to these decisions, the fact remains that the EU chooses these images. We can either ignore that it does so and tell ourselves that it is meaningless, or we can at least question the motives. The EU has a programme of expansion beyond countries we associate with Europe. Former president of the European Commission, Romano Prodi, stated that "Europe's time is almost here. In fact, there are many areas of world affairs where the objective conclusion would have to be that Europe is already the superpower, and the United States must follow our lead."

It should not be surprising then, that the cold war mentality is being adopted by this evolving superpower. There have been repeated attacks made by the MSM and various European and national politicians against Russia, particularly in terms of the way its culture and social ethics are rooted in Orthodox Christianity. The EU Parliament produced a resolution called Strategic Communications in the EU as Opposition to the Propaganda of Third Parties. Not a title likely to be quoted in the press very often, much less remembered by the public. The resolution accuses Russia of challenging western values, and amongst the weapons of this attack the resolution names the Russian Orthodox Church. As the liberal social agenda gathers pace, organisations identified as maintaining traditional morality are to be viewed as enemies.

As the economic demands imposed by the EU cripple those countries unsuited to the German model of finance, observers have suggested a potential collapse of the EU structure, but this is to fail to see the true picture. As indebted countries are forced to sell off their resources, as German bankers swoop in and collect their prizes at a fraction of their true value, the EU is also undermining the democratic choices of those nations. Rather than being a risk to the EU, the financial disasters provide an opportunity for the removal of elected leaders and in their place the positioning of men committed to the EU programme at the expense of national interests.

The illusion of democratic accountability is maintained by heated debates in the European Parliament between elected MEPs. But in reality power does not lie with them but with the senior staff running the departments who operate in over three thousand working groups on which no MEP is permitted to sit. The budgets for these groups are not disclosed, their sources of income are equally secret, and the extent of their powers is never revealed. Their complete lack of accountability to any of us demonstrates the real contempt for people of Europe.

The EU has been granted by the UN the same status and rights as national governments; it now has the authority to submit proposals and amendments to UN laws and resolutions. Its standing on the world stage has the full backing of the Roman Catholic Church, indeed Pope Francis is one of its most outspoken supporters. All of this is an indication of the direction we are travelling in, something we can only truly understand by setting it in its historic context. The Roman Empire had a single currency, a single emperor, a single army; it was a pagan empire that governed peoples of many nations and languages. Monet's dream of a single, unelected government that is unaccountable to the people it rules is almost here, it is the rebirth of the old Roman order, established not by the sword, but through stealth and bureaucracy.

Chapter 5 ~ Freemasonry

In late 2016 I was working as a secondary school teacher and had a surprising conversation with another member of staff. She told me that during the holidays she had returned to school to complete some marking but had been told by the caretaker that she could neither enter the school building nor even use the car park because the Masons were using the hall. I later caught up with him and he assured me that not only was it true, but that they had insisted that all the security cameras in and around the hall had to be covered so that nothing they did was seen or recorded. My concern was not put to rest when the secretary of the school assured me that they only met on school premises for an annual dinner: the level of secrecy was clearly out of proportion for what they claimed they were doing. My only other encounter with them had been at Anglican theological college some years earlier. My room-mate had revealed to me that he was a Freemason, and admitted that because of his poor academic record he had only managed to be accepted for training for the ministry because the Director of Ordinands in Manchester at that time was also a member.

There are different arguments as to when Freemasonry began, some claim it started in the

Middle Ages, which has not been proved, but there is concrete evidence that it was in existence by the 1600s. We have accounts of initiation rites from 1646, and by the early 1700s four London lodges combined to form the Grand Lodge which even by this point had published its rule book. Over the next hundred years there was a rapid expansion of Freemasonry around the world, and by 1814 it is believed that there were six hundred and forty-seven lodges in existence. This had grown to nearly three thousand by 1900; with Grand Lodges also being established to rival that in London. The trauma experienced during the two world wars created a great deal of spiritual confusion, and just as there was at this time a rise in interest in spiritualism so too Freemasonry attracted many thousands of new members. In 1967 the Royal Albert Hall hosted the 250th anniversary of the creation of London's Grand Lodge, during which His Royal Highness the Duke of Kent was installed as Grand Master. Other notable Freemasons have been Kings Edward VIII, Edward VII, George VI, Winston Churchill, Benjamin Franklin, Andrew Jackson, George Washington and a host of figures from the worlds of politics and entertainment. It is estimated that there are approximately six million Freemasons today, with two Grand Lodges now set up for women.

The lower ranks of Freemasonry consist of what are called three degrees; they are the Apprentice degree, the Fellowcraft degree and then the Master Mason degree. Many Freemasons claim that this is the limit of their hierarchy and yet there are numerous Masonic publications referring to at least thirty-three degrees, while some writers make the claim that there are even secret degrees beyond these. As a member is initiated into each degree he receives secret teaching known only to men of his rank and makes an oath to protect the secrecy of these teachings on fear of brutal punishment and death. Those of higher degrees receive teaching that reveals the inner meaning of the symbolism, rituals and language of Freemasonry, much like Gnostic devotees who are given sacred lessons as they progress. Members of the highest degrees are described as being "illumined" since they have been granted the means of drawing closest to the light.

On their own London website the Freemasons accuse those who criticise them as confusing their "secular rituals with religious liturgy". They argue that they are a society of like-minded men who perform acts of charity, and as we shall see, many of those at the lower levels of Freemasonry do indeed believe that they belong to an organisation that is nothing more than this. However, material produced by the Freemasons themselves makes it clear (in fact states quite openly) that the true nature of Freemasonry is not only concealed from those outside of its ranks, but from those in the lower orders too.

During the late 1800s there were many immigrants to the U.S.A. who found belonging to some kind of fraternal order a way of establishing business and social links, and so groups like the Elks Club, the Lions Club and many others grew up. There is nothing sinister about these organisations, they simply gave outsiders a way of connecting with others, although even members of these groups have been accused at times of favouring fellow members in matters of business. With so many men belonging to these types of organisations, it was often assumed that Freemasonry was merely a larger version of what they knew to be benign. However, while this is a perception the Freemasons have been keen to promote, it is false: Freemasonry is an occult organisation opposed to the Church and its teachings. Freemasonry teaches that salvation is not achieved through Christ alone, but through a collection of esoteric practices, many of which are satanic. For example, only as members advance through the degrees of Freemasonry are they exposed to the teaching that there are two gods, one of whom is Lucifer, and that it is Lucifer who is good while the other, Adonay (Adonai), is evil.

This concealment of its true nature is achieved through a deliberate misleading of lower level members through a complicated series of rituals and imagery. Language is carefully manipulated so as to conceal their true doctrines, for example the term "Grand Architect" might satisfy a Christian that it is God the Holy Trinity Who is being worshipped, without there ever being an explicit reference to Christ. This is why Freemasonry advocates ecumenism, teaching that all religious texts are of equal worth; it is the rejection of the exclusive claims of Christianity. In a number of Masonic publications it is stated that one of their goals is the unification of all religions around a single altar where men of every faith will worship the one true god.

Many of the beliefs of Freemasonry have been embellished over the years but essentially they consist of a mixture of Old Testament stories and Ebionite Christianity (Ebionites were an early Christian-Jewish sect) combined with pagan and occult beliefs. The stonemasons' tools form the basis of much of their symbolism, the square and compass suggesting the emphasis on reason and responsibility, but as we shall see in our next chapter, Freemasonry also draws on a number of ancient cults for its ideas. It is no coincidence, for example, that the George Washington Masonic Memorial in Alexandria, outside Washington D.C., sits beneath a tower that is fashioned after the ancient Lighthouse of Alexandria in Egypt.

Much of what we know of the real nature of Freemasonry comes from a Masonic handbook called "Morals And Dogma of the Ancient and Accepted Scottish Rite of Freemasonry", compiled by Albert Pike in 1871 (which was presented to every Freemason reaching the fourteenth degree until 1974). On page 624 Pike states that "Masonry is identical to the ancient mysteries"; the subject of the next chapter in this book. As Pike says, from the very beginning of their membership Freemasons are repeatedly told to "seek the light", a phrase that might assure a Christian that what they are doing sits comfortably with their faith. However, Pike makes clear that it is Lucifer who is the light-bearer, or more specifically, the one who bears the light of Freemasonry. Pike reinforces this by printing on the cover of the original volume the Latin phrase "Deus Meumque Jus" which means "God and My Right". To the uninitiated the very fact that it mentions God will assure them that all is well. In fact the term is taken from Satanism; it is the claim that the one they worship will grant them their rights and justice on earth.

Throughout the book Pike refers to the practices of Freemasonry as "the craft". This is a term for witchcraft and continues to be used amongst Freemasons in their texts today. It is typical of their approach to use names most people are unfamiliar with but to those with the knowledge they are an open acknowledgement of what they are doing. According to Anton LaVey in the "Satanic Bible" there are known to be seventy-seven names used in

Satanism for the devil. For example one of these is Baphomet who the ancient Gnostics taught was the fiery appearance of the Holy Spirit, personified by Satanists as the Goat of Mendes. Baphomet is portrayed as a hermaphrodite and is the god of sex for many witches, but also openly seen as a representation of Satan by others. Another example is Typhon, a name often quoted by Blavatsky who we mentioned earlier in relation to Alice Bailey. Typhon is identified as an Egyptian god, and is typical of the way Freemasonry claims to have its roots in ancient faiths while at the same time claiming to be secular in nature. It was through the networks of Freemasonry and Theosophy that the New Age movement came into being, the very concept comes from Masonic literature. There was even a Masonic magazine called "New Age Magazine" but the title was changed because it was seen to be making too clear the link between Freemasonry and the New Age occultism that has become so popular in the West: few New Agers would be comfortable knowing their "enlightened" ideas came from Masonic halls.

It is not surprising that those who abandon Christianity also reject Christian morality. Freemasons must swear to their willingness to lie in order to protect their fellow members. On page 183 of the "Masonic Handbook", compiled by Edmond Ronayne, we find the instruction that "You must conceal all the crimes of your brother

Masons". On the same page it states that "if you live up to your obligation strictly, you'll be free from sin". We see here the nature of Masonic morality; above all else the Freemason must be obedient if they are to be judged sinless. On page 74 it states that "whenever a minister prays in the name of Christ in any of your assemblies, you must always hold yourself in readiness, if called upon, to cut his throat from ear to ear". Again this savage act, the handbook states, will achieve a sinless state if it is performed in obedience. In the early degrees, an exception is made for treason and murder, but this absolute obedience is demanded of those in higher orders.

If the Freemasons restricted their activities to ensuring employment in one another's companies we might consider it unfair, but hardly worthy of great concern. However Freemasonry has spread its influence far beyond these kinds of parochial matters. In 1981 a right wing lodge of Freemasons called Propaganda Due (or P2) was discovered to have been involved in illegal action. The Italian press uncovered the names of over a thousand members which included high ranking figures in politics, business, banking and the Italian intelligence service. The government of the day tried to suppress the story and as a result Arnaldo Forlani's party lost power. It is interesting to note that the Euro MP Mario Borghezio stated that he hoped members of the Italian government were "independent of the occult powers which control Europe". As mentioned earlier, the Duke of Kent is the Grand Master of the United Grand Lodge of England, and it is his personal assistant, Andrew Palmer that organised the Bildeberg conference when it was last held in the U.K. (in Turnberry). Another of his duties has been to organise secret conferences of leaders of various oil and banking cartels: it should come as no surprise that Bildeberg and these other secret groups are linked to the Freemasons.

In his book "Inside the British Army" Antony Beevor states that there have been periods when the Army Board has consisted only of men who were Freemasons. This should be of concern since the Board makes decisions about ranking and promotion in the British Army. Its thirteen members include the Secretary of State for Defence, the Minister of State, the Chief of the General Staff, the Commander in Chief for Land and the Adjutant General.

Evidence of the influence of the Freemasons came to light after the tragic murder of sixteen primary children and their teacher in Dunblane in 1996 by Thomas Hamilton. A hundred-year public secrecy order has been placed on one hundred and six documents relating to the case. The argument put forward was that since the case involved young children, the documents should not be made public. In fact only a very few of the documents mentioned the children, and the Sunday Herald has unearthed a very different motive for the secrecy. The documents include letters sent between Labour and Conservative ministers relating to Hamilton's involvement with the Freemasons. Amongst them are letters from George Robertson, the then head of NATO, and Michael Forsyth, then Secretary of State for Scotland. A further secrecy order was placed on documents relating to a report from 1991 about Hamilton's involvement in child sex abuse.

Further influence has been exerted through endowment formulations which have helped to shape much of American educational, financial and foreign policy. These foundations have been the source for many advisers and actual officials for many U.S. administrations. One of the most influential of these has been the Council On Foreign Relations which has guided many U.S. regimes in its dealings with the rest of the world: its membership also consists primarily of Zionists, a subject to be discussed later. Another example is the Federal Reserve which, contrary to popular opinion, is a privately owned bank which controls the U.S. economy.

There are now twelve Masonic lodges dedicated entirely to senior police officers. For example lodge number 9719 was established by the West Mercia force (covering the U.K. counties of Herefordshire, Worcestershire and Shropshire) in the town of Craven Arms. The Master of the Lodge at its dedication was the Chief Inspector of Shrewsbury. We should rightly ask how we can have confidence in a legal system where members of the police force belong to secret organisations. Police officers have denounced arguments that membership should be made public on the grounds that it might raise doubt about their evidence in court or the reliability of disciplinary hearings. When the government proposed to investigate the matter, Lord Millet (a law lord and Freemason) said such enquiry would be "oppressive". It is a matter of public knowledge that many members of the House of Lords are Freemasons including the following who have all gone on trips abroad on "Masonic business": The Earl of Eglinton; Lord Barnard. Lord Cornwallis; Lord Franham; Lord Lane of Horsell; The Marquee of Northampton; Earl Cadogan; Viscount Chelsea and many more (an extensive list was published in Punch magazine).

Membership alone is not sufficient proof that the Freemasons are seeking to protect their vested interests. But in 2000 the BBC programme "Southern Eye" uncovered evidence demonstrating how Freemasons were using their positions on councils to influence planning decisions according to their benefit. The investigation found links between councillors, building companies and solicitors firms and was able to prove that members' interests were being protected and promoted illegally in Portland.

But even proof of corruption might not come as any real surprise to most people who instinctively recognise that there must be a reason for wanting to maintain a group's secrecy as the Freemasons do. For the Christian however, Freemasonry is unacceptable and has been condemned not just by individual Orthodox bishops, but by whole councils and by the Church as a whole. The condemnation of Freemasonry has been expressed in the strongest possible terms and there can be no doubt that no Orthodox Christian should ever join the Freemasons or remain one if he has joined in the past. A commission of members of all the autocephalous Orthodox churches met on Mount Athos (at the Monastery of Vatopedi in June 1930) and identified Freemasonry as a "false and anti-Christian system". The official statement of the Church of Greece (in 1993) stated that "Freemasonry is not simply a philanthropic union or philosophical school, but constitutes a mystagogical system which reminds us of the ancient heathen mystery-religions and cults from which it descends and is their continuation and regeneration". The bishops went on to state that "Freemasonry is a direct offspring of the Egyptian mysteries". The bishops noted that this is demonstrated in their initiation ceremonies; the bishops also observed that the rituals of

Freemasonry are of a blasphemous and anti-Christian nature.

The bishops recognised that beyond the specific details there is also an underlying nature to Freemasonry which is in opposition to Christianity. It is a syncretistic system that presents itself as being tolerant of all other religions while actually maintaining its superiority to them. Through its promise of moral perfection through knowledge of truth it leads its members into the worship of foreign "gods" by declaring itself to teach only "natural truths" which can be discovered through the rational mind: it rejects the very concept of Christian revelation. The bishops of Greece condemned Freemasonry for its claims of offering the means to redemption. Orthodoxy maintains that there can be no perfection of man outside of Christ.

This welcoming of all faiths brings any Christian Mason into a new brotherhood with atheists, Muslims and any other faiths, while Christians who are not Masons are reduced to a secondary relationship with them: Freemasonry demands that the true allegiance of its members is not to the Body of Christ but to other Freemasons. As Father Ingram Irvine wrote, in his letter of 1917 objecting to the appointment of Aftimios Ofiesh to the episcopacy because the latter was a Freemason, "If a bishop of the Church is a Freemason then every priest in his diocese had better be a Mason, for otherwise it will follow that a Jew, an infidel, an atheist etc. or the lowest saloon keeper, or house of ill fame manager, as a member would have more influence as a Mason with the Masonic bishop than the priest who was not a member of the order."

In "Introduction to Freemasonry" Carl Claudy celebrates the fact that a Freemason may "in his private petitions pray to God, or Jehovah, Allah or Buddha, Muhammed or Jesus. In the Masonic lodge he hears petitions to the Great Architect of the universe, finding his own deity under that name." There is a great deal of evidence that the ecumenical movement is founded on Masonic principles which have as their ultimate objective the stripping from men's minds the belief that there is anything unique about Orthodoxy. I have no wish to enter into the scandal of the accusations made against certain patriarchs and I feel I have no right to use their names here without absolute certainty of their membership, but the Masonic Grand Lodge of Greece claims that there are some bishops who are Freemasons, and a simple cross-reference reveals that they have all made positive statements about or been directly involved with the ecumenical movement.

The bishops who have denounced Freemasonry have done so because they recognised it as a false religion. In its rituals Freemasonry conflates the identity of Christ with Mithra, Hindu deities, Mahdi of Islam, Isis and the Jewish Kabbalah. Furthermore Christ is redefined by Freemasonry according to its natural or rational system which is really no more than a form of pantheism. This resulted in The Holy Synod of Bishops of the Church of Greece in 1996 calling Freemasonry "a congregation of the Antichrist" because it denies the saving truth given to the Church. The higher degrees of Freemasonry contain teachings entirely based on the Kabbalah (as described in publications of the Grand Lodge of Athens) and it is as a whole an occult system that uses images and symbols to re-enact a promise of resurrection by means of a Godless philosophy. Man is elevated above all, as Albert Pike writes "God is as man conceived him, the reflected image of man himself". For Freemasons it is man's own reason that is of absolute worth, and while Pike dismisses Christian interpretation of the Bible as "vulgar" he proclaims man's reason as the source of God. Freemasonry promises self-understanding to its members who are taught through allegorical plays which are learned and acted out within the lodge. Freemasonry claims that through these rituals the allegories hidden within all the world's religions are made clear, and so Freemasonry sees itself as the ultimate rational science which contains everything needed by man. In short, Freemasonry deifies rationalism.

Freemasonry defends itself with claims of being no more than a secular organisation and insists that it is being persecuted by those who seek to unveil its true nature, but their secret influence over politics is being concealed beneath the outward show of doing charity work. It is a means of secret influence within governments, international banking, the courts and our workplaces. But Freemasonry seeks to normalise itself in the mind of the public, even recently launching a "roadshow" through the shopping centres of Kent to educate people and assure them that there is nothing to be concerned about. But Freemasonry is a secret network of powerful and influential men who make decisions about some of the most important aspects of our lives. Furthermore it is an occult organisation that has at its heart an anti-Christian system of belief that is driving the attack on Orthodoxy. Its makes clear its longing for a single temple which will one day be built to welcome the whole world in a unified religion, something Christians recognise as the foundation of the coming Antichrist's rule. So long as Christians remain true to their faith they remain the enemy of Freemasonry. It is only the Church which has had revealed to it the warnings about what is to come, and so those working for evil view faithful Christians as a threat to the hidden agenda which they promote. So many of the Masonic predictions and plans are now coming to fruition, the variety of religious sects and their willingness to unite is the harvest Freemasonry has been working towards for a number of centuries. Before looking in detail at the Masonic movement called ecumenism, let us examine these ancient cults from which Freemasonry takes its beliefs in order to see the true nature of their craft.

Chapter 6 ~ Ancient Cults

The focus of this chapter will be to examine how Freemasonry has used the structures of ancient cults and mystery religions in its attempts to present itself as the continuation of these ancient secret teachings. From them Freemasonry has adopted the same distinction between the elite minority which is granted access to inner teachings and the wider majority which is presented with simplified interpretations. We will consider a few examples of these cults and identify the similarities between both them and with modern secret societies.

The Freemasons use the words of Saint Paul to account for their secrecy; they take his teaching that the immature must be fed with milk while those who have grown to spiritual adulthood can feed on meat, as an indication that certain teachings should be hidden from the majority of people. This kind of manipulation of texts is typical of the Masonic approach, one that is applied not just to Christian texts but to any teaching that can be reshaped to fit their purposes. The argument put forward by Freemasonry is that even in ancient pagan times, it was understood that few people are capable of the kind of philosophical reflection that is needed to understand the true mysteries of nature and life. With these select few the true mysteries were shared, while the majority were given stories of gods who represented the natural forces and energies that the Masonic elites believe are at work in the universe. It is control of these forces and participation in their actions that forms the basis of magic and various occult practices.

Of course, one benefit from this approach was that those who had access to the secret knowledge could join together in exclusive fraternities, and it is clear that special social status and political influence always accompanied such membership. Much of this teaching was communicated through ritual dramas performed within the group, which is from where the Freemasons take the idea. Accompanying these teachings were threats of punishment against members who revealed the secrets, including death threats. So seriously were these taken that the philosopher Plato declined to join certain groups because he wished to write publicly about the ideas and membership would have required him to remain silent.

The claim of Freemasonry today is that the major religions of the world are nothing more than watered down versions of the real teaching, and that though most of these ancient mysteries have been lost, the few that have survived are maintained within the higher Masonic degrees. But more than this, their belief is that it is only through the maintenance of this secret knowledge that humanity has been able to make the advancements it has in science, philosophy, art and every other intellectual endeavour. Freemasons are taught of the high moral value of their organisation, and of the great benefits it has brought to humankind.

One of the reasons Freemasonry is so opposed to Christianity (though this is never made explicit to members of the lower degrees) is because the pagan mystery cults were themselves in opposition to the Church from the earliest times. The use of what pagans called "divine magic" was recognised by the early Church as demonic occultism, but there was a more philosophic argument. The mystery cults taught that it was only through the individual's growth in virtue and moral goodness that the individual was made worthy to receive the secret teaching. The Christian call to recognise our personal sinfulness, and that through this recognition of our fallen nature we are able to receive God's mercy, was repugnant to the pagans: they argued that morality is not only linked with but is dependent on knowledge. It is the very basis of salvation which is at stake here, since the cults taught that an intellectual perception of nature and her laws is crucial to the ability of man to think intelligently and become moral; and without this he remains unsaved. The Freemasons use this philosophy to claim that their concern is for the improvement of man, since they have incorporated this doctrine of morality being dependent on knowledge.

93

Christians also rejected these cults because so many of them practised worship of the sun. In many of the mystery cults we find the sun deity represented in human form, often with the sun's rays symbolised by long golden hair. It is interesting that many major companies today include the image of the sun or the sun's rays in their corporate logos (such as Shell Oil, Suntrance and Columbia Studios). We should remember that these logos are designed with great care, often costing tens of thousands of dollars, with every aspect being carefully scrutinised: it is no coincidence that the sun is so prevalent within them.

Very little written evidence has survived of these cults and so there has been a great deal of speculation about their beliefs and practices. It is this absence of hard evidence that has permitted the Freemasons to fill the vacuum with its own interpretations and explanations. For example, in the twentieth century there were many self-appointed experts who claimed that Christianity was influenced ritually and doctrinally by these groups, and though there is clear evidence to show the open hostility between Christians and pagans, many texts have reprinted the claims as though they were factually correct. In this way a new (and false) orthodoxy is being established, feeding into the fantasies of Freemasonry. But we know that in 395 A.D. Emperor Theodosius outlawed these pagan practices and demanded that their temples be destroyed: it was through his efforts that many of the mystery cults had died out by the fifth century.

We will now consider a few examples of these mystery cults in order to both understand more, but also place in context the teachings of Freemasonry. Most of these cults were concerned with fables which involved a ritual re-enactment of death and rebirth in some form. The stories focussed on the activities of deities and for the cult members the main message was of hope in a better afterlife. One of the earliest examples was the Eleusian cult, which is thought to have been in existence in the sixth century B.C. (though Masonic writers claim that it dates back to the fourteenth century B.C.). In Athens a great procession took place during which the ritual drama was played out of two goddesses, and it was taught that participation in the rite would transform the individual both intellectually and morally. For the general population the cult presented itself as being about the cycles of nature and particularly the harvest, but the more esoteric teachings have now been lost. Freemasonry argues that the Eleusian cult had great influence on Plato and that it is through his teaching that its principles have survived to this day.

The Eleusian cult had the typical demarcation of teaching between what they called the "Lesser" and "Greater" knowledge. Their central image was of a divine tree of which the members were seen as a mystic fruit. Freemasonry claims that the secret teachings concerned esoteric interpretations of various Greek myths which revealed the true science of nature, though there is insufficient evidence for this argument. But the principle that many initiates should participate without really understanding the true purpose is taken by the Freemasons as having a longstanding tradition which in no way indicates deceit.

Another feature of Freemasonry that is based on claims about the Eleusian cult is the ritual accompanying the swearing to secrecy. Masonic writers describe Eleusian oaths which declare oaths of secrecy upon penalty of death if they were broken. This creation of an ancient history is used to give authenticity to modern practices and may assure contemporary candidates that what is being demanded of them is simply part of this tradition. Such histories also dignify what otherwise might appear threatening and bizarre.

A cult which is often linked to the Elusian beliefs is the Bacchic Mysteries. Once more we discover ritual plays relating teachings about death and resurrection and again the members were divided into two groups, according to their level of initiation. Another group, the cult of Dionysos shared many of the Bacchic beliefs (some scholars maintain that their deities were in fact the same being) and interestingly the members were primarily drawn from the building trade and architects. Freemasonry has often claimed that it was they who built the Temple of King Solomon described in the Old Testament (despite not being Jews or worshipping the God of the Jews which makes the claim highly unlikely). Freemasonry also attributes the building of many other ancient monuments to themselves and that evidence of this is to be found in symbolic inscriptions carved into their stone. They do not accept that their organisation has simply adopted the symbols they have found in such works.

Perhaps one of the most familiar deities amongst these cults was Isis, whose worship in Rome probably began around the second century B.C. and reached its peak of popularity in the second century A.D., but had spread through the Greek world as early as the fourth century B.C.. Isis was another goddess associated with the harvest and her devotees believed that she bore a son with the Egyptian deity Serapis, called Harpokrates. This is worth mentioning because depictions of Harpokrates show him with one finger raised to his lips to demonstrate the secrecy of the cult. In contemporary culture we can find a number of pop stars photographed performing the same gesture (no doubt at the behest of those controlling them) as a shared acknowledgment amongst those who are initiated into modern versions of the cult that those behind the images are of a common mind.

The cult of Isis was based largely on Egyptian practices and the members saw themselves imitating the rituals of the Egyptian priests. Like modern Freemasonry, only men were initially permitted to become priests but later women were accommodated. Freemasonry reflects the organisation of the cult of Isis in that members made progress through a series of initiations which enabled them to learn higher levels of teaching. We also find this in the cult of Mithraism which had seven grades of membership (Mithraism was of Persian origin but spread throughout the Roman Empire due to its popularity amongst Roman soldiers). One aspect of their rituals copied directly by Freemasonry is that at entry to the first level of membership candidates were given a crown to wear while having the point of a sword held to their chest.

British Freemasons claim to have links with the Druids despite there being no real evidence as to their beliefs or practices (Druidism today is a modern invention having no links whatsoever with the ancient Druids that lived here so long ago). Freemasons make the claim that Druids were sun worshippers, which is as likely as anything else, although we do know that when the Romans invaded Britain they were surprised to find worship of Roman deities such as Apollo, Mars and Mercury, which would suggest that the Druidism that existed at that time was not native to Britain (or that they simply incorporated different deities into their belief system much in the same way as Hinduism has). There is some evidence that Druids were divided into three classes, and like the other mystery cults, secret knowledge was only shared with the highest class. It has been suggested that the Druids believed in a form of purifying suffering after death, much like Roman Catholics believe about purgatory, but much of this remains speculation. In August 2004, the then Anglican Archbishop of Wales, Rowan Williams, was inducted into the highest level of Druidism and given the Bardic name Ap Aneuri.: he later became the Archbishop of Canterbury. This fact may reflect how far these groups have travelled in becoming accepted by wider society; and even by some Christians!

The real point of conflict between these pagan groups and the Christian Church came through the heresy of Gnosticism. The Gnostics incorporated pagan beliefs into their interpretation of Christian doctrine, and the Freemasons portray them as just one of the many branches growing forth from the main trunk of the Christian Church (the "Branch Theory" will be considered in our next chapter). But the early Church rejected any possibility of Christianity being mixed with occult philosophies and various pagan versions of astrology. Gnosticism presented a universe where absolute spirit and absolute substance exist alongside one another, and that Christ the divine "nous" could not have been crucified as that which is absolute spirit cannot die. Instead they argued that Simon the Cyrene was crucified in His place, in the same way that Islam later taught that a substitute died in Christ's place.

Perhaps the most well-known name of any secret group today is the Illuminati. It has its roots no further back in time than 1776, when its founders are believed to have set out to gain as much political and social influence as possible by having members appointed to important posts. There is a great deal of speculation and hysteria surrounding this particular group, but what we do know is that from the beginning the plan was to limit church involvement in public life. Like the Freemasons, the Illuminati adopted a number of symbols to declare their presence and intent, many of which are clearly of occult origin (such as the all-seeing eye seen on the CBS logo and the incomplete pyramid where the missing capstone may equally represent the unfinished plan of the organisation or the one who is yet to take complete power of all others. The headquarters for the Supreme Council of the Southern Jurisdiction of the Scottish Rite of Masonry is similarly capped by an unfinished pyramid).

The intention here has been to demonstrate how Freemasonry draws on the ancient mystery cults for its doctrines but also show how it uses the great age of these groups to authenticate its own practices. The groups it draws from have a clear anti-Christian bias and have always been condemned and rejected by the Church. The notion that Freemasonry is no more than a secular club whose aims are charitable works and the betterment of its members is nonsense, and even the motives for its charitable work should be questioned. In February 2017 Canterbury Cathedral hosted an international Masonic service, presided at by the Dean of the cathedral, the Rt. Revd. Robert Willis. When asked why he had permitted such an event, the Archbishop of Canterbury, Justin Welby, explained that it only seemed right to let them use the cathedral because they had previously donated £300,000 towards the repair of the North-West Transept. There was no mainstream media coverage of the event.

Chapter 7 ~ Ecumenism

Ecumenism is the intention to establish intercommunion between all Christian groups, regardless of doctrinal differences. The syncretistic beliefs of Freemasonry find their expression in the ecumenical movement and as we shall see, it is Freemasons who have been behind the promotion of ecumenism. We must acknowledge that many sincere Christians have been seduced by the language used by ecumenists when they speak of overcoming quarrels to achieve "union" between all Christians, but we shall recognise how empty such terminology really is, and what the true objectives of this movement mean for Orthodoxy.

The term "Ecumenical Movement" was first used in 1920 to describe the strengthening relations between Christian groups. The World Council of Churches (W.C.C.) was formed in 1948 (the same year as the United Nations Charter for Human Rights was published) when two earlier ecumenical groups, "Faith And Order" and "Life And Work" joined forces. We must acknowledge that the Ecumenical Patriarch (of Constantinople) played an important role in the early years of the movement though Russia played no role at this stage because it was under persecution from the communists (in the 1970s however, as Father Seraphim Rose recorded at the time, the Soviet State sought to force the Russian Orthodox Church into active membership of the W.C.C. in order to destroy its uniqueness in the minds of the Russian people).

The establishment of The World Council of Churches was financially supported by the Rockefeller Foundation which first appointed John Foster Dulles to lead the National Council of Churches in America. Dulles was a member of the Council On Foreign Relations and also chairman of the Rockefeller Foundation Trustees. Dulles was sent to the founding conference of the W.C.C. in Amsterdam in 1948 to promote the Rockefeller strategy. It had been recognised that not only Orthodox, but also Roman Catholic and Evangelical Christians were opposed to the idea of doctrine being treated as secondary to the idea of outward unity at any cost. And so the Rockefeller plan was to establish a new idea that would speak over theological differences; this was what became known as the "social gospel". By encouraging Christians to focus primarily on collaboration to help others, it was understood that they would quickly form social and organisational bonds that would become stronger than the content of the faith they professed. Christians were taught to focus on social justice as the primary aim of their response to God, which enabled the replacement of traditional Christian spirituality with a worldly, materialistic version of Christianity. Serving our neighbour has always been a fundamental Christian concept, but now it was to be the main purpose of Christianity. In this way, any objection raised about doctrinal differences could be portrayed as disruptive and creating disunity which threatens the social action of the ecumenists.

A further example of how major corporations are promoting this agenda is the case of Rick Warren and his Peace Coalition. Warren, another member of the Council On Foreign Relations, was the Protestant minister invited to pray at Obama's presidential inauguration and was described by CNN as "America's pastor". Warren produced a contemporary version of the social gospel idea in his book "The Purpose Driven Life" and subsequently received a two million dollar donation from Rupert Murdoch to promote his vision: his book sold over thirty million copies in the U.S..

The aim of these organisations is to redefine the purpose of being a Christian. Through the use of the new language ("tolerance" and "acceptance") the insistence on truth becomes "divisive" and even "unloving". But Orthodoxy teaches us that it is not a man-made unity that God desires but one founded on a common faith in the revealed truth of Christ. We cannot create unity amongst the different Christian groups by pretending that there are no differences. The very idea of creating utopia on earth is misguided at best, but the ecumenical understanding of "union" is itself flawed. It assumes that the Church is divided and requires bringing back together as one. This contradicts the Orthodox teaching that Christ's Church was created at Pentecost through the descent of the Holy Spirit, and remains one until Christ's second coming. Those who have separated themselves from the Church have not created additional "churches", they have simply left the Church. The divine gift of the Church's unity is in need of no restoration, the Church continues in the fullness of its faith and sacramental life.

Faced with this doctrine the Protestants created a new theology which was able to satisfy their wish to believe in their continued participation in Christ's Church. This is the "Branch Theory", a claim that the thousands of Protestant sects with their different doctrines are all branches growing from the one trunk. This heresy was rejected too by the Roman Catholics until they adopted their new ecclesiology at Vatican II which recognised these other groups as "churches". In order for a union to exist amongst these many denominations it was necessary to reduce the Christian faith to its lowest common denominator on which the groups could all agree: while Orthodoxy teaches the essential nature of the fullness of revealed truth, ecumenism requires the jettisoning of those doctrines which it identifies as "secondary" and unessential for salvation. This enabled the ecumenists to side-step the incoherence of Protestantism, and find agreement on the bare bones of what was shared. But this stripping down of the faith also makes the next step in the ecumenical agenda possible: the broadening of this "union" beyond the Christian sects to embrace people of every faith. Since the kind of Christianity that is espoused within the W.C.C. is devoid of real Christian doctrine it became much simpler to make the leap to the idea of a shared spiritual impulse experienced in different forms and beliefs. The W.C.C now openly proclaims its mission as being to respond to the multifaceted, pluralistic nature of religious belief, and its goal is to establish a new fellowship of all human beings, not just of Christians. The consequence has been for a number of contemporary Roman Catholic and Protestant scholars to question the absolute need of Christian faith for salvation: in fact many have begun to suggest that traditional Christology may be a barrier to full and open dialogue with other faiths. In January 2016 the Vatican released a video in which Pope Francis denied the essential differences between faiths, stating that all world religions are "seeking God or meeting God in different ways." The video includes shots of representatives from many different religions, and the Pope went on to describe Christian fundamentalism as a "sickness" which denied the essential similarity of all religions.

The union of all religions is spoken of at length in Father Seraphim Rose's book, *Orthodoxy And The Religion Of The Future*, but things have progressed quickly and dramatically since he was writing. A union of all religions is now spoken of openly by international organisations. The European Union is funding a project called "Soul For Europe" which maintains that no one religion should be considered to have "more truth" than any other, and that just as is taught in Freemasonry, all religions have grains of truth which can nurture our spiritual lives. This false religion seeks the counterfeit spirituality of the Gnostics and the mystery cults; it maintains that all religions have the same source and goals. It is interesting to note that one of the principle bridges between many Roman Catholics and Protestants has been the charismatic movement. This phenomenon offers Christians of any sect the opportunity to by-pass the intellectual self in what it claims is a powerful experience of the Holy Spirit. Unlike traditional and biblical accounts of the work of the Holy Spirit, charismatics do not have to struggle with matters of falsehood or truth, nor are they prompted to repentance, but instead enjoy states of elation and exhibit "signs" of their spiritual encounter. In fact we can see the same manifestations of these states in many pagan religions around the world, and whatever spirit is entering them it is not the Holy Spirit. But Roman Catholics and Protestants take this experience as evidence that God is calling people beyond the divide of doctrine, and it is taken as proof that God is calling Christians to a new kind of unity. This trusting of the spirits is destructive, it is based on the ignorance and foolishness of its followers who assume that all spiritual experiences must be good, that feelings of elation can come from no other source but God. When we see charismatics barking like dogs and acting as though intoxicated (because that's how it must have been at Pentecost!) we can only shudder at the devil's trickery. As we shall see in a later chapter, these are manifestations of the New Age deception that has swept through the western world.

That the ecumenical movement, and specifically the World Council of Churches, are part of the Freemasonry attack on Orthodoxy, may still appear fanciful to some. So let us consider what the Masons themselves previously stated quite openly but which they now deny or attempt to conceal. In the 1962 edition of the Freemasonry magazine Le Symbolisme we read: "Do not let people say, my brethren, that Freemasonry is the counter-church. This was only a phrase suited to the occasion; basically, Freemasonry wants to be a super-church which will bring all churches together in her bosom."

The foundation for this super-church is not a single shared faith, but that through tolerance and respect of one another's doctrines, Christians will see their connection and loyalty to the group as more important than their belief. Observing the new ecclesiology established in Roman Catholicism through Vatican II, the Freemason Yves Marsaudon summed up this philosophy as Unity in diversity: a phrase that could just as easily have been coined by the W.C.C.. The ultimate aim of a single world religion is never far from Masonic writings on religion.

The charismatic movement reflects this Masonic ideal, it is the establishment of a common experience that is capable of being shared with people of any faith. Masonic literature points to an ultimate religious experience called *theurgy* which is a form of spiritism which has its origins in Egyptian cults claiming to offer communion with unseen deities. By exposing people to a profound and deeply "religious" experience the intention is to make the individual's feelings more important than the revealed truth of the Church. Today we see a growing emphasis on our inner sense of truth, children are taught in schools to find inner fulfilment and the likes of Oprah Winfrey have espoused this dogma for decades. The new consciousness has been carefully crafted in the West to prepare people for this common religion, but it can only be successful when a sufficient majority of people have abandoned authentic Christianity. As we look at the changing nature of Anglicanism and the various western forms of

Christianity, it is not alarmist to suggest that the task has nearly been completed.

We must see ecumenism and the charismatic movement as rooted in paganism, the paganism of Freemasonry: as Marsaudon wrote: "Ecumenism is the spiritual son of Freemasonry". Through the use of appealing terminology, such as world peace and brotherly love, the conscience of Christians is subdued into accepting pagan practices, and those who object are labelled as zealots and fanatics. By making man himself the final arbiter of truth, and through the subtle inclusion of the rituals of the mystery cults, the "god" that is worshipped is not the Holy Trinity.

For many Orthodox Christians the situation is complicated by the apparent approval of ecumenism by some bishops. Therefore we will now focus on how ecumenism has been treated by the Orthodox Church and the warnings that have been issued by the monastic community on Mount Athos.

Up until the nineteenth century the Orthodox Church unanimously and unequivocally followed the apostolic and patristic teaching that the Orthodox Church is the One, Catholic and Apostolic Church which alone professes the fullness of faith revealed to man necessary for salvation. In 1865 the first seeds of change were planted when the leadership of the Theological School in Haiki was given to Filotheos Vrynios who had studied theology in Germany. The change can be traced in the dogmatic creeds published from this time onwards which adopted a far more open stance to the heterodox West. The School's teachings reflected those of the Phanar and marked a decisive change in attitude towards Rome and the papacy. There are three main documents, published by the Ecumenical Throne in 1902, 1920 and 1952, which both reflect but also establish the change in outlook: let us briefly consider each of them.

The Encyclical of the Ecumenical Patriarch (1902) instituted a new tone in its attitude to the West which allowed the Phanar to recognise the ecumenical movement as a positive phenomenon. But even in this document the heterodox were still referred to as "tendrils", they would not be elevated to the status of "churches" until the Encyclical of 1920, which was the first time the Ecumenical Patriarch of Constantinople had addressed heretical groups as such, and which enabled a further change. The Encyclical declares that dogmatic differences should be no barrier to communion between the Orthodox and the heterodox. In a single stroke the blood of countless martyrs was declared spilt in vain, and the words of Saint Paul are ignored when he says "what communion hath light with darkness?" (2 Cor.6). The document claims the "love between churches" demands that the Orthodox make no attempt to convert the heterodox since it will only create "bitterness". The basis for these relations is clearly not to enter dialogue in order to share the Orthodox faith but to compromise doctrine so that a worldly union can be established. In 1948 the "Resolution of the Conference in Moscow against papism" declared papism "anti-Christian" and the patristic teachings about Rome were confirmed. However, by 1952 the Ecumenical Patriarch was willing to ratify Orthodox membership of the W.C.C. under the guise of "transmitting to them the wealth of its faith, worship and organisation". We can trace this thread through to 1993 when the infamous Balamand decision was made to recognise the heresy of Rome as a "sister church" (this statement was never accepted by the Orthodox except by the Romanian Orthodox Church). In these few documents we see the growth of syncretism which has resulted in the refusal at Balamand to condemn heresies; we see the hand of Freemasonry at work even in the Church of God.

In the face of all this there have been numerous Orthodox voices that have spoken out in opposition to these ecumenist trends. We shall focus on two of them: the responses from Mount Athos and a powerful letter addressed to Pope Francis from two Greek bishops which articulates the traditional voice of the Church.

In April of 1980 there was an "Extraordinary Joint Conference of the Sacred Community on Mount Athos". The purpose was to address the

Orthodox involvement in the ecumenical movement with particular reference to the dialogues with Roman Catholics. In the document it released the Orthodox position was made clear: the heterodox Christians of the West have "perverted the Faith of the Gospel", and that those confessions outside of Orthodoxy are "deprived of sanctifying grace, of real mysteries and apostolic succession." As Saint Basil the Great also said, "Those who have apostatized have no longer on them the grace of the Holy Spirit". Therefore, the Athonite fathers concluded, dialogue with the heterodox must only have one goal: to enable heretics to return to the Orthodox Church. The statement also emphasised that there should be no common prayer or joint services between the Orthodox and heterodox until oneness of faith is attained. To do so will only risk confusing the faithful who may begin to imagine parity between them. This statement was signed by representatives of all twenty monasteries on Athos who noted their own removal from the influence of secularism and "scholastic Western theology".

In 1999 the Holy Community felt it necessary to send a letter to Patriarch Bartholomew to voice alarm at the increasing links between the Ecumenical Patriarch and the Pope. Rejecting Pope John Paul's claim to Rome and Orthodoxy being the "two lungs" of the Church, the fathers reminded the patriarch that any union with Rome would be false so long as the latter held on to her heretical doctrines. The fathers stated that "it is totally impossible to consider heterodox Rome as being one of the most holy Orthodox local churches" and that participation by the patriarch in pan-religious common prayer was the cause of grief to the Holy Community. Recognising the true outcome of ecumenism the fathers added that: "Common prayer stands against the commands of the Old and New Testament as well as the Holy Canons, as they prepare the way for the pan-religion of the so-called "New Age".

In 2014 two Greek bishops, Andrew of Dryinoupolis, Pogoniani and Konitsa and Seraphim of Piraeus and Faliro wrote to the Pope to call him to repent of his errors and remind him of Rome's heresies. First they made it clear that Roman papism is not a "church" but a worldly organisation governed by the Pope. This, the bishops stated, was no less than what the devil offered Christ in the wilderness: earthly rule in return to allegiance to him. They called him to renounce the theological errors of Rome: a) the Filioque; b)created grace; c)papal infallibility; d)baptism by sprinkling and its separation from chrismation; e)the use of unleavened bread in the Liturgy; f)the refusal to give Holy Communion to children; g)the dogma of the immaculate conception of the Theotokos; h)the belief in purgatory; i)belief in the superabundant merits of the saints; j)the compulsory celibacy of

114

the clergy; k)the legalistic interpretation of "original sin"; l)the rejection of Holy Tradition; m)the juridical character of the mystery of confession and n)the Uniate which has been the cause of so much suffering of Orthodox peoples.

The bishops point to the election of Pope Francis as being the will of international bodies concerned with the financial situation in South America who intend to use his interventions to ensure their own interests are protected. Behind these bodies are the Freemasons who openly anticipated his appointment, as the Monastic Grand Master G. Raffi stated "With Pope Francis, nothing will be as it was before. It is a clear choice of fraternity for a Church of dialogue." The bishops go on to refer to ecumenism as the "religion of Lucifer" and reject any false union with "churches" that will not reject their heresies. The true intention of Rome is revealed in one of the so-called revelations from "Our Lady of Fatima" who promised the Roman faithful that "The Holy Father will consecrate Russia to me". This denial of the faith of Orthodox Russia reveals the true nature of these visions and the extent of the deception over so many Christians under Rome's yoke.

There have been many attacks on the Church through the centuries of its existence, and often the worst of these has come from outside of it. But with ecumenism we see the Church being attacked from within: while claiming to "unite the Church" the ecumenists divide it. Or rather they threaten to separate Christians from it, since the Body of Christ cannot be divided (though it can be wounded). By attacking the Church's understanding of itself the ecumenical movement undermines its foundations in order to weaken it before the coming of Antichrist. We see the spirit of ecumenism in so many areas of human life; it is the charge of relativism, the fruit of pluralism that denies objective truth. Without discrimination or "testing of the spirits", many well-meaning Christians are mixing false beliefs and practices into their faith (let us remember that orthodoxy means true belief and practice). The centuries have seen so many martyrs die in their refusal to deny Christ even in the smallest way, but today the attack of Satan is hidden, and the evil is made to look good, while the good is portrayed as evil. No Christian can exist in isolation; our life is dependent on membership of Christ's Body. Where ecumenism prevails, the truth is lost and the individual is cut off from the tree, bearing no good fruit. But let us not lose heart or feel afraid, let us recall the words of saint John Chrysostom who says: "Nothing is stronger than the Church...if you fight against a man, you either conquer or are conquered; but if you fight against the Church, it is not possible for you to win, for God is the strongest of all" (in his homily prior to being exiled).

Chapter 8 ~ Zionism

Zionism has become a problematic issue to discuss because Zionists themselves have managed to manipulate the discourse surrounding it in order to present critics of the Zionist project as anti-Semites. The successful merging of the perception of "Zionism" with "Judaism" has prevented many from daring to analyse the reality because politicians and journalists know that once someone has been branded with the "anti-Semite" mark there is no coming back: this in itself speaks of the degree of power and influence Zionists have over modern culture in the West. But the truth is that millions of Jews have been the victims of Zionism, and there are in fact millions more Christian than Jewish Zionists. There are countless Orthodox Jewish rabbis who reject Zionism as a fundamentally evil movement and, as we shall see, they base their objections firmly on the teaching of their faith. Zionism is a nationalistic and racist movement that has been willing to sacrifice Jewish and Palestinian lives in order to achieve its political aims. We will look at the historical development of Zionism before recognising its impact on the world; we will then consider why so many U.S. evangelical Christians have joined this movement. Finally we will reflect on the broader issues relating to the state of Israel.

The Zionist movement arose in the late nineteenth century and today has two basic aims: to create a Jewish majority in Palestine and so achieve a statehood which does not recognise the political or national rights of the indigenous Palestinian people. Zionists taught that the Jewish people have an inherent and divine right to the land of Palestine. Two hundred years ago Jewish communities were fragmenting; there was a crisis of identity amongst many Jewish people which had been created by events from the previous century. Anti-Semitism had resulted in two responses from Jewish communities: while some withdrew into isolation others attempted to adapt their traditions and beliefs to the then prevailing cultures of Europe. The French Revolution brought about a new opportunity for Jews to participate in a wider range of employment and social activities, many converted to Christianity, and there was a weakening of Jewish religious belief and practice. It was this growing secularisation of Judaism that allowed the Zionist leaders to emerge with a new, non-religious concept of belonging and identity. By the 1870s groups were appearing who argued that only through the establishment of a Jewish homeland in Palestine could the Jewish people regain their national identity.

One of the early strategies was to encourage large scale emigration of Jews from around the world: the immediate effect of this was to raise the Jewish presence in the Palestinian population from six to ten percent from 1880 to 1914. Recognising what was happening; Christian and Muslim leaders urged the government in Istanbul to help prevent Jewish land purchase and further immigration. The response was for the Zionist Congress in 1905 to call for increased "colonisation" of Palestine, leading to even greater fears amongst the Palestinians. In 1914 a meeting was arranged of Palestinian and Jewish representatives, at which the Arabs and Christians hoped to have a detailed explanation of what the Jews wanted and how they intended to integrate with the indigenous people: the Zionists refused to reveal their plans.

Two factors at this time were to enable Zionist aspirations to be met, both involved Britain. The first was the British occupation of Palestine and the other was the need to entice the U.S.A. into the First World War. The British government felt able to treat areas of the Middle East as its own, particularly as its troops were stationed in Palestine. It wouldn't be until the signing of the Treaty of Versailles at the end of the war that the Germans would discover how their defeat had been achieved through Zionist plotting. In November of 1917 the Balfour Declaration was signed by the British promising Palestinian land to the Jews: it would not be until 1948 that the agreement was finally fulfilled. With a German victory too likely, Britain negotiated with the Zionist owners of the

U.S. media in order to persuade the American people of their moral duty to support entry into the European war; Palestine was simply the bargaining chip. The Declaration gave emigration to Palestine a boost since British forces were seen to be defenders of the Jewish immigrants. By 1936 the Jewish presence in Palestine had risen to twenty-eight percent of the population and in the next ten years would reach thirty-two percent. A huge number of land purchases were permitted under British rule and Zionists were permitted to buy into Palestinian natural resources, including the supply of electricity to the whole of Palestine except for Jerusalem. Jews were encouraged to employ only other Jews, increasing Palestinian unemployment and poverty. When Arabs rebelled (in 1920, 1921, 1929, 1936 and in the late 1940s) the Zionists refused to seek negotiated settlements but always turned to violent suppression.

In 1947 the United Nations stepped in, offering a deal that gave the Jews statehood in fifty-five percent of Palestine, much of which still had an Arab majority living there (the UN effectively endorsed the segregation desired by the Zionists). Although the Palestinians rejected such proposals, once the British forces withdrew from Israel, in 1948, Zionists proclaimed the state of Israel. By 1949, amidst the last echoes of the war, the Arab areas of Palestine had been reduced to just twenty-three percent of their homeland and the issue of

Palestine itself was no longer seen as a local Middle Eastern problem but now as part of the world-wide Jewish question. The Zionists insisted that indigenous Palestinians should leave the Jewish state, but when they refused to leave their land, leaders such as Ben-Gurion demanded that they be forcefully removed at British tax payers' expense.

One of the most important figures in the Zionist movement was Theodor Herzl, whose ideas shaped much of the direction it would follow. Herzl is a hero for many Zionists, but in fact he was a racist who portrayed the Arabs as inferior and dangerous. Zionists promoted the idea that Jews were part of a superior European culture, and in 1886 Herzl wrote in the Jewish State that the Jewish presence in Palestine could act as "a wall of defence for Europe and Asia, an important outpost of civilisation against barbarianism."

For Herzl and his contemporaries Zionism was simply nationalism. A homeland was seen as the only way Jews could re-establish themselves on the international stage of economic and political affairs. The settlement programme was always understood to be a key weapon, and it is no surprise that in its infancy it was financed by the likes of Baron Edmond de Rothschild who also supported the First Zionist Congress in Basel, Switzerland, in 1897 which had a long term plan which was subsequently carried out over a number of generations. Herzl believed that to combat anti-Semitism in Europe was ultimately impossible, and so he promoted the vision of separation. Assimilation had failed, he argued, and so when Zionists took control of Palestine there was never any intention of integration with the Palestinians. As soon as it was possible segregated schools were established and the Hebrew language was used as a means of dividing the population. It is ironic that, as schools in the U.S.A. were being desegregated, Zionists were enforcing a new segregation amongst the children of Palestine (even more so when we note that the famous case of Brown Vs Board of Education in 1954 which made integration possible in U.S. schools was passed by the Supreme Court by a vote of nine to nothing: eight of these were Freemasons the ninth was a Zionist Jew).

From its early inception Zionism made clear its intention to eventually exclude indigenous Palestinians in order to eventually create an Israeli state that could annex the West Bank and Gaza. What we see in today's Middle East is really the exercising of what was called the Yinon Plan (after Oded Yinon who was attached to the Foreign Ministry of Israel), a plan to balkanise the Arab states surrounding Israel, including Syria, Lebanon, Jordon and the Sinai, in order to weaken them. Iraq was always understood by Zionist strategists to pose the biggest threat to their expansionist plans and the Yinon Plan makes clear the need for a war

122

between Iran and Iraq to destabilise the two states. Israel's development as an imperial power was dependent on first dividing the surrounding area into warring factions: we can see the success achieved in Iraq but thanks to Russian intervention, Syria (at the time of writing this) remains resistant to the plan.

Herzl, in his diaries, wrote that the "Greater Israel" would extend from the Nile to the Euphrates (while some have claimed that the two blue lines on Israel's flag represent the design of the prayer shawl, others argue that they represent these two rivers). This version of an expanded Israel has appeared on Israeli coins, and in his July 1947 speech to the United Nations Special Committee of Enquiry, Rabbi Fischmann described the same plan and included Syria and Lebanon in the territories to be given to Israel. It is remarkable how open the Zionists were at this stage of history: today we hear nothing of this plan from Israeli politicians.

Yinon has identified Israeli invasions of Lebanon and other Arab states as providing the ideal conditions for displacing Arabs from the region, in fact he went as far as describing likely peace treaties as potential problems for Zionist expansion. Yinon also made clear that those Arab states which have a strong social structure and secure government should be targeted most forcefully since they pose the greatest obstacle to the plan. In fact the destruction of Arab states appears repeatedly throughout Israeli strategic thinking, Yinon described these states as "a house of cards" built by foreign states such as Britain and France in the 1920s, and therefore as having no credible legitimacy or history. Within this fragile structure Yinon identified the division between Shia and Sunni Muslims as a potential means of destabilisation, and many observers today point to the military conflicts in the Middle East as the fruit of this strategy. By creating a region torn apart by wars the Zionist plan was/is to establish Israel as the only dominant state capable of establishing peace through its military strength.

There has always been Jewish opposition to Zionism, chiefly from the Orthodox rabbis. Rabbi Gedalya Liebermann warned all Jews to distance themselves from the movement because it demonstrated disloyalty to God. He explained that Judaism is, and always has been, a religion, not, as the Zionists were claiming, a race or a nationality. From the promises of God, Liebermann insisted that no Jew should leave exile through his own efforts, but patiently wait for God to act. To enter Israel ahead of time, he said, was an act of rebellion against God. For Liebermann and other rabbis the claim to be able to interpret the scriptures and decide on the future of the Jewish people could never be made by politicians since they lack the qualifications necessary to interpret holy tradition or God's word. The founders of Zionism were never experts in the Jewish Law, nor did they have the spiritual authority to lead the Jewish people, and as Rabbi Teitelbaum wrote, such claims made by Zionists proved them to be "the work of Satan" and "a blasphemy". For Orthodox Jews the Torah is the source of Jewish identity, and whoever denies the faith and the Torah is not a part of Israel. Zionists proclaim a state to be the source of Jewish salvation whereas the rabbis teach that people can be saved by God alone. A further concern is the pragmatic reality that the actions of Israel will only create more anti-Semitism for those faithful Jews living elsewhere in the world. The bigger picture was summed up by Rabbi Moshe Aryeh Friedman when he said "The existence of the Zionist regime is based upon the belief that they have to destroy belief in God throughout the world. Another one of their goals is to destroy other peoples, both physically and economically...By fabricating lies about the Holocaust, global Zionism has succeeded in distorting historical truth in its favour...Hollywood succeeded in influencing global public opinion." (In a 30th September interview on Channel 2 of Iranian T.V.).

But the arguments from the rabbis focus on the historical behaviour of the Zionists too, since their disregard for human life in order to achieve their goal was not limited to Palestinians. The organising of the international boycott of German goods in 1933 was a deliberate provocation intended to force

125

the issue for those Jews living comfortably in Europe. In 1938, President Roosevelt convened the Evian conference which was intended to address the Jewish issue. When the Germans agreed to allow Jewish people to leave Germany for two hundred and fifty dollars per person, the Jewish Agency representatives chose to ignore the offer, condemning millions of Jews to persecution and death.

In 1941 the Gestapo offered to transport German Jews either to Spain or to the British colonies, but the Zionist politicians refused the offer on the grounds that they would not be permitted to travel to Palestine. A similar offer was made in 1944 concerning the Hungarian Jews, but again only emigration to Palestine was seen as acceptable to the Zionists living safely in Switzerland and Turkey. A further example demonstrates the lack of concern the Zionists felt for other Jews. In December 1942, visas for three hundred rabbis were made available by the British government to enable the clerics and their families to escape to Mauritius. Once more the offer was declined by Zionist leaders because only Palestine was acceptable as a destination. These situations were repeated many times, and each time the Jews were denied safe passage because the Zionists did not want Jews travelling anywhere but to Palestine. Perhaps the most infamous example was in February of 1943 when Romania offered to allow seventy thousand Jews to leave at a price of just fifty dollars a head. The story received coverage in the New York press and so when Zionists once more refused to allow life to be saved, Yitzhak Greenbaum, Chairman of the Rescue Committee of the Jewish Agency, was forced to defend their actions. Greenbaum dismissed the concerns and insisted "one should resist this wave which pushes Zionist activities to secondary importance." To confirm that the state of Israel was more important than the lives of individual Jews, Greenbaum added "One cow in Palestine is worth more than all the Jews in Europe".

A key aspect of the Zionist plan is to maintain military and economic support from strong allies, without which the state of Israel could never have survived. For many years this was the role played by Britain, but from the 1940s it was the U.S.A. which bankrolled Zionism. Through a tightly controlled media the image is maintained of an Israel which always intends to achieve good, while accounts of slaughter and injustice are portrayed as errors of judgement. The U.S. Neo-Conservative politicians maintain that a strong Israel is good for U.S. interests because it ensures the presence of a powerful (nuclear) ally amongst potential "rogue" states. But American support for Israel goes beyond this shallow politics; it is rooted in the heretical beliefs of many evangelical Christians. The Pew Research Centre surveyed thousands of churchgoing Americans to gauge their attitudes towards other religious groups: it revealed that evangelicals had a profoundly positive attitude towards Judaism and the Jewish people. This has resulted in Christian Zionism becoming a huge and dangerous lobby group, including organisations such as the Christian Zionist Organisation, Christian Friends of Israel and Christians United for Israel. Christian Today magazine completed another survey which revealed that one in four U.S. evangelicals believe it is their biblical duty to support the State of Israel. Interestingly, while this attitude exists amongst the evangelicals, amongst the more traditional denominations more concern was expressed for the plight of the Palestinians. But the surveys reveal that there are approximately fifty million American Christians who feel this support for Israel in comparison to around only five million Jewish Zionists. It is worth noting that indigenous Christians in Israel have repeatedly voiced their opposition to Zionism, and in 2006 Patriarch Michel Sabbah added his voice to the Heads of Churches in Jerusalem in a statement which read "We categorically reject Christian Zionist doctrines as a false teaching that corrupts the biblical message of love, justice and reconciliation. These policies advance racial exclusivity and perpetual war."

This support for Israel can be traced to a number of sources, both political and theological. In nineteenth century Britain there emerged a Protestant movement which taught that Christians must establish a Jewish state in Israel in order to make possible the second coming of Christ. Christians were taught it was their divine duty to recognise the link between their eschatological hopes with the Jewish homeland: for many, the events of 1948 only confirmed these beliefs. At the 2007 American Israel Public Affairs Committee, Pastor John Hagee (who leads an evangelical community of nineteen thousand and is broadcast regularly on radio and television) announced to those present that "The sleeping giant of Christian Zionism has awakened. There are fifty million Christians standing up and applauding the State of Israel."

The heretical foundation of these attitudes is the teaching that the Jews remain God's chosen people. Certainly this is the claim that continues amongst Jews themselves, but for two thousand years the followers of Christ have understood the new Covenant in Christ Himself which established a new Israel: the Church. It is those who have the life of Christ within them that are God's people, while those who still await the messiah reject Christ's divinity as do the pagans and atheists. But dispensationalism teaches that the Jews maintain a unique position outside of the Church, a teaching that has never been accepted by the Orthodox Church.

Since they are seen as God's chosen few, the evangelicals teach that the Jews have an exclusive claim to their "homeland", which is why so many of them have lobbied for the U.S. embassy in Israel to be moved to Jerusalem: a suggestion repeated by Donald Trump within weeks of taking office. This reduces the Palestinians to a level of unwelcome aliens in their own land, something about which the evangelical Zionists have little concern. But as the Prophet Micah writes: "What does the Lord require of you, to act justly, to love mercy and to walk humbly with your God." (Ch.6 v.8)

Another basis for Christian Zionism was the deliberate misinterpretation of biblical texts. In 1909 the Scofield Reference Bible was published by Oxford University Press which included notes to the texts which stressed the Zionist interpretation that it was God's will that the Jewish people be in possession of Palestine. This resulted in many American evangelicals falsely believing that this was the traditional and orthodox meaning of the Bible. They were genuine in their desire to be faithful to God, but they were misled by Jewish scholars who were behind the publication (In his book The Incredible Scofield and His Book, Canfield demonstrates that Zionist bankers financed the publication).

As a result of these influences the modern concept of Judaeo-Christian was born, yet another example of the way language is manipulated to control the way we perceive reality. In America there are evangelical groups who have incorporated Jewish practices into their worship, such as blowing the shofar (ram's horn) or lighting the menorah. It results from a lack of connection with Christian tradition; an attempt to recreate a link with a past they believe existed before the birth of Roman Catholicism. But it also stems from a complete misunderstanding of what modern Judaism is; so long as it is linked with the faith of the people of the Old Testament and even Christ Himself, then we are in error. Even to apply the term "Judaism" to the ancient tribe of Israelites is a mistake. Time and again in the gospels we read of Jesus coming in to conflict with the Pharisees and Scribes. This was not just because they were failing to live up to their faith, it was because they were the first signs of a new faith: two religions were coming into existence at this time, Christianity and modern Judaism. The "tradition of the elders" that the Pharisees referred to was the as yet unwritten form of what would be the basis of the Talmud. Saint Paul's criticisms of the Jews' "man-made religion" were not aimed at the faith of the Old Testament, but to what was becoming "Judaism" (a term never used in the Old Testament). Only after the fall of the Temple in Jerusalem did Rabbinical Judaism subvert the faith of the Jews according to Talmudical teaching. At the heart of the Talmud is a shocking and blasphemous reality: it is not God

131

Who is worshipped but the Jewish people themselves. The Law of Moses has been replaced with the law of the Talmud, as Jesus said "teaching for doctrine the commandments of men". Jesus warned that this new, oral tradition (at that time) nullified the commandments of God, it created a tradition of hypocrisy. The Pharisees claimed that this oral tradition was given in secret to seventy elders (from which we get "Sanhedrin") who sat at the base of the mountain while Moses received the written (and inferior) Law. Once the Jews were taken into Babylon they needed a system that could maintain their identity now that they had no access to the Temple. After the destruction of Jerusalem in 70AD it was this form of the religion, taught by the Pharisees that became the dominant authority in Judaism. For over a thousand years Babylon was the home of the majority of Jews, and much of its beliefs entered the Talmudic traditions. For example the Talmud assures its followers that there is no sin committed if a man has sex with a child under the age of three: a reflection of the practices of the Babylonian cults. When it came to writing this oral tradition down, many slanders were inserted about both Christ and the Theotokos, and all non-Jews were determined to be less than fully human (the goy). It is important to recognise that modern Judaism is not simply an incomplete version of the Old Testament faith, or a slightly altered version that cannot accept God's Messiah: it is a complete perversion of that faith that rejects and nullifies the faith of the Old Testament. The evangelicals that insist that there is still some biblical foundation to Judaism are in error, they seek to accommodate apostates, but in doing so they incorporate false teachings into their own faith. Evangelicals assume that the modern Jewish perspective should be applied to the Bible, but in fact it is the tradition of the Church itself which is the only key to a true understanding of the texts. Evangelicals who promote the idea of modern Jews still being a special people have embraced the religion of the Pharisees which Jesus so frequently condemned. The Talmud maintains that the Bible is incomplete, and that only through the use of these Rabbinical teachings can the deficiency be overcome (this is ironic considering the Protestant heresy of sola scriptura – that all that is necessary for salvation is contained in the Bible). The very Pharisees who rejected God's Messiah were the same men who produced the Talmud which would become the new faith of the Israelites. The Roman Catholic scholars who translated and distributed Latin versions of the Kabala were corrupting both their own faith and that of the Protestants who would be born of them. But Christ's warnings are so utterly unacceptable in our politically correct age that few Christians dare repeat their meaning and fewer evangelicals even understand how far they have been deceived. This new idolatry (the

133

Talmud) states very clearly that "the Babylonian Talmud represents God in the flesh". Such is the confidence of modern Judaism that Rabbis have begun to admit openly that the Talmud describes Christ as a sorcerer, a sinner who performed black magic and a sexual pervert who was sponsored by external powers in order to subvert the people of Israel: the fact that evangelicals have been so blinded to reality is a sign of how powerful the Zionist control is over the media, education, language and even perception of reality.

But there is a further aspect to Zionism which remains hidden from most discussions about its origin and nature: Freemasonry. The link between Zionism and Freemasonry is something kept hidden from those in the lower degrees, and such an assertion requires evidence. We shall look at what both the Zionist Freemasons themselves have written but also the signs of how the two are connected in the Masonic rituals and symbols.

There are a large number of Masonic lodges that permit only Jewish members, and the B'nai B'rith Lodge is where the Anti-Defamation League sprang from. The A.D.L. has an enormous influence on the U.S. government and its links with the Zionist media ensure that it is capable of destroying the reputation of anyone who opposes it. But let us turn to the evidence itself. As Rabbi Isaac Wise wrote: "Freemasonry is a Jewish establishment, whose history, grades, official appointments, passwords and explanations are Jewish from beginning to end." We also find The Jewish Guardian stating in April 1922 "Freemasonry is born out of Israel." And in the July 1928 edition of the Masonic magazine Le Symbolisme we read "The most important duty of Freemasonry must be to glorify the Jews, which has preserved the unchanged divine standard of wisdom." And in a 1927 editorial of the Jewish Tribune we find "Freemasonry is based on Judaism. Eliminate the teachings of Judaism from the Masonic ritual and what is left?"

In Israel today there are believed to be approximately sixty Masonic lodges with around three thousand members. In the U.S.A. there have been fifty one Grand Masters who have been Jewish: a disproportionate representation when we remember that Jews make up only three percent of the U.S. population. But we must be careful not to assume all Jewish involvement in Freemasonry has been Zionist in nature. Amongst the immigrants to the U.S.A. and in post-revolutionary France, many Jews saw membership at the local lodge as a sign of acceptance after a history of being refused participation in the full spectrum of social and economic life of Europe. Therefore it is arguable that many Jewish men will have chosen to become Freemasons because it offered a kind of emancipation. However, this does not adequately explain the level of influence Judaism had on Masonic culture.

One of the fundamental ideas in Freemasonry is the Temples in Jerusalem, both that of Solomon and the Second Temple which lasted until A.D.70. (the columns of the Masonic halls are symbols of the Temple columns). The rebuilding of the Temple is a key Zionist aim (one that will necessitate war in the Middle East since the site is presently occupied by the Dome of the Rock, Qubbat As-sakhrah, the mosque marking the second holiest site in the Muslim world). Solomon too is a fundamental character in Masonic mythology and his name is recalled in a number of their rituals. Again, many of the oaths sworn by Freemasons are drawn from the Talmud, and Masonic terminology, legends, symbols, and even the Masonic coat-of-arms used by the Grand Orient Lodges of England and Europe are distinctly Jewish. In Scottish Rite Freemasonry, all official documents are dated according to the Jewish calendar using the Hebrew months and year according to the Jewish era. We also find many examples of Hebrew being used, and above all, we see a direct parallel between Masonic philosophies and the teaching of the Cabala (secret occult teachings that some Jews believe were given in ancient times and preserved – just as in the other mystery cults).

It is not surprising that both Freemasons and Zionists are reluctant to be so open about the links between the two groups. But in the 1900s Gougenot de Mousseauz was able to collect a very large number of documents that demonstrated, without question, that Zionism was at the core of Freemasonry. In his book Lejuif, Lajuaisme: et la Judaisarion des Peoyles Chretiens (published in 1869) he was able to state that "The real chiefs of this immense association (Freemasonry) are mostly Jews, and live in close and intimate relationship with the militant members of Judaism, those namely, who are leaders of the Cabalist section. This is known to only an intimate few in Masonry."

The philosophical consequences of the natural sciences so beloved by Freemasons (described previously) are rooted in Zionism. We find a desire to remove Christianity from all areas of public life, such as the government, education and all public institutions. The removal of crosses in American schools and of prayers before local government meetings in the United Kingdom are examples of this and the removal of the religious understanding of marriage in order to encourage access to divorce (this secularisation of marriage and its effects on social stability is considered in detail in a later chapter). We see the promotion of secular humanism as a basis for state education in order to reduce Christianity to one more system amongst many. And using the language of inclusivity and tolerance once more, extending the freedom of religion to any belief system, which requires cults such as the Jehovah's Witnesses or even Satanism, as worthy of respect. The attack on Christianity and traditional Christian values is at the heart of Zionist Freemasonry, since it sees an imperial Israel one day becoming the great power in the world. Many Zionist groups in Israel give financial support to immigrant support groups to enable large scale migration of Muslims into Europe (while refusing them entry into Israel). The goal is to destabilise what remains of a Christian continent, and through the destruction of the Christian majority enable the demographic impact to reduce the influence and presence of the Christian faith. As we shall see later, authentic Christianity is the real enemy to this movement.

It has been noted that approximately eighty percent of the U.S. Senate is now completely supportive of Israel (and of the remaining twenty percent few would be brave enough to voice their concerns over Israel's actions). The U.S. government is heavily influenced by Freemasons who consider upholding Zionist interests more important than the safety of their own country. Rockefeller Standard Oil and the various Zionist banking groups now dominate the U.S. government and its relationship with the rest of the world. In Russia Freemasonry was suppressed because it was recognised as undermining the Tsarist system, and it was understood that the Masons had benefited from the revolution in France as well as other disorders which had occurred across Europe. The Russian revolutionary leaders were principally Zionist Freemasons. When the lodges had first appeared many joined and considered themselves "freethinkers" – this was really a term for rejection of God and monarchy. From the very earliest history of Freemasonry its members have been involved in conflict with the clergy and many have spoken out at the influence and power of the Church. Of course, in almost all of these cases it was Roman Catholicism they were rebelling against, but from their viewpoint this was the only Christianity they knew. It is worth noting that this particular conflict may be coming to an end, Grand Master G. Raffi stated that "With Pope Francis, nothing will be as it was before. It is a clear choice of fraternity for a Church of dialogue."

A number of U.S. presidents have invested their time and reputation in seeking a supposed resolution to the issue of Israel and Palestine. There has been talk of a two-state solution, giving power to determine their lives to both Jews and Palestinians. But rarely do we hear talk of a one-state solution: creating a future for Palestine based on the ballot box. Israel refuses to accept democracy because the Palestinians out-number them by three to two. Just as in the apartheid of South Africa, it is a ruling minority which refuses to share power with the oppressed majority. But the real threat to Zionism that the one-state solution brings is the possibility of complete integration of Arab and Jewish populations, which would guarantee Palestinians legal status as full citizens, something Israel utterly rejects. One thing Israel can never permit is the diversity it demands of other nations. The media will never state that Palestine can either be Jewish, or it can be democratic: it can never be both.

The treatment of Palestinians is really the fulfilment of the teachings of the Talmud which permits Gentiles to be treated as less than human. But this fact must not be used as an excuse for anti-Semitism. The reality is that most Jewish people we meet in our lives are, just like the lower degree Freemasons, innocent of the crimes committed by Zionist elites. In fact, many will be ignorant of the international nature of the movement for a single world religion and government, and as has been described, many Jews have been sacrificed by the Zionists to achieve their goals. But those people outside of Israel, especially in the U.S.A. are sustaining the Zionist agenda when they offer uncritical support for what is happening to the indigenous people of Palestine. The media is creating an atmosphere hostile to Muslims, and Zionists are keen to manipulate us into understanding Israel's attack on Palestinians as a conflict between a democratic nation and Muslim terrorists. Israel kills three Palestinians for every one Israeli that dies, and this ratio extends across the decades to 1948: but the mainstream media does not present it this way. Let us now turn our attention to some of the ways in which the Zionists are managing the world's economy and how the banking industry is being used as a tool of oppression.

Chapter 9 ~ Banking

We have seen how secret societies, Zionists, and the military industrial complex all play their part in affecting the world and our lives: unelected, unaccountable groups who determine international events and national policies. But behind all of this are the international bankers who pull the strings. In this chapter we will see just how the bankers control governments, destroy international economies when it serves their own ends, and how they are working to create a system of control that will result in economic slavery of every person on the planet. These statements may sound exaggerated, perhaps even extreme to some, but the overwhelming evidence for these claims is undeniable. But let us begin with a brief history of how the European bankers took control of America.

In the seventeenth century the first colonists who had escaped to the New Continent to seek religious freedom, found that they were still paying heavy taxes to the banks back in Europe. One of the chief recipients of these taxes was the Bank of England which had spread its influence into North America through the Hudson Bay Company. In response, to escape the clutches of the banks, the colonists began printing their own money (in 1690). This new currency had no basis in a gold or silver reserve, and prompted outrage from the House of Commons which recognised an attempt to escape taxes. In 1742 the British Resumption Act was passed which forced all state governors to end the use of the new currency, which resulted in a widespread depression in the colonies. This gave the British government the opportunity to seize land from the colonists at a tenth of its value, sowing the seeds of resentment. It is worth noting that in his autobiography, Benjamin Franklin wrote that the Revolutionary War of 1776 was in response to the British king's refusal to allow the colonists to determine their own currency rather than tax on tea or anything else that later became the official narrative. When America won its independence from King George's rule, it was able to form its own government, but the Rothschilds and other Jewish gold traders still held the reins to America's finances through the continuing debt that had never gone away. Thomas Jefferson wrote: "Slavery to a military force can be abolished by an opposing force of arms. But a debtor's enslavement to a creditor, no weapons can overthrow."

The new American government was forced to introduce taxes on the colonists in order to pay off the European banks, and this was the opportunity for the bankers to act. In 1791, Alexander Hamilton persuaded congress to create the First Bank of America through the Assumption Act of 1791. This new financial institution was chartered by the Bank of England in a contract lasting twenty years, and so the European bankers took control over the people who had fought to be released from their taxes. At the end of this twenty year period the Americans tried to escape from the charter which resulted in British troops sailing into Washington in 1812 and burning down both the White House and the Treasury Department Building. Once more the American people believed they had won a war with the British, but the cost of the conflict resulted in President James Madison creating the Second Bank of the United States, which again was chartered by the Bank of England (which had eighty percent ownership) and which once more ensured money flowed across the Atlantic to the Rothschilds and others.

By the 1820s, President Andrew Jackson was elected on a promise to abolish the bank, which he managed to do as well as paying off the debt. This resulted in fierce opposition from European bankers who made an attempt on his life - mainly because he had passed into law that it was unconstitutional for any private interests to print American currency. We can see a pattern emerging when, in 1865, President Abraham Lincoln was assassinated for refusing to accept credit from the Rothschilds at eighteen percent interest, and instead had issued "green-backs", which were interest-free. Again, in 1881, President James Garfield made a stand against usury banking (the charging of interests for loans) and was assassinated by a known Freemason. In 1901, President William McKinley became known as an advocate of "hard money" (asset-based loans), he was assassinated and succeeded by Theodore Roosevelt, another known Freemason.

Perhaps the greatest blow to American economic freedom came in 1913, when a Jewish consortium had its private bank signed into law by President Woodrow Wilson, as the Federal Reserve. Immediately the "income tax" was introduced, giving the European bankers a continuous source of revenues from American workers. The largest shareholders are the Rothschilds, with fifty-seven percent of stock which is never made available for trading on the stock exchange).The Federal Reserve became the puppet master for America's national and international policy, for example leading the nation into the First World War, and securing the Balfour Agreement described earlier. By the 1930s, President Franklin Roosevelt, another Freemason, was requested by the bankers to remove the gold backing of the dollar, which he did, changing the very nature of American money to a system of debt (which we shall examine later). As Napoleon once said: "When a government is dependent for money upon the bankers, they and not the government leaders control the nation. This is because the hand that gives is above the hand that takes. Financiers are without patriotism and without decency."

Economists are all familiar with what is called the "Rule of 70" for interest. This is the system that states that if the prime rate is seven percent then the money on loan for that interest doubles every ten years. In other words, it enables the banks to double their money every ten years – paid for by the public. While the banks are owned by national governments, this money goes back to the nation, but the reality now is that it becomes profit for international bankers.

It is not just presidents who have been eliminated. In 1933, Congressman Louis McFadden tried to bring impeachment charges against the Federal Reserve Bank; he was poisoned three years later. In 1963 President John Kennedy was questioning why the American people were paying interest on their own money supply. The Federal Reserve was now issuing the nation's currency (despite the laws passed under Andrew Jackson) for its own profit. Kennedy put an end to the borrowing of Federal Reserve notes and instead issued United States notes. Kennedy was assassinated in Dallas and once in office President Lynden Johnson returned America to Federal Reserve notes. But the bankers recognised that they still could not exert complete control over the nation's economics so long as U.S. coins still contained precious metals, thus giving them an

146

actual worth. Johnson was persuaded to remove all silver from American coins, which finally released the Federal Reserve from having to link the dollars they printed to anything real: they had become nothing more than proof of credit. The words of Meyer Rothschild echoed through the years, he said "Give me the right to issue a nation's money, and then I do not care who makes its laws." The illusion of governance, concern with the petty rules under which we live is as nothing compared to the whole-scale theft of a nation's wealth.

The Federal Reserve is a consortium made up of nine Zionist controlled banks which are ultimately controlled by the Rothschilds. These nine banks are controlled by The Rothschilds, the Lazards, Israel Moses, the Warburgs, the Lehmans, Loeb Kuhn and Goldman Sachs. Its system for making profit is very simple, it prints and then loans money to the U.S. government for which it charges interest. So the American people are charged by a private banking group for the privilege of having a currency. Whenever there is a financial crisis (unlike in Iceland where many bankers were jailed and the economy is now recovering), most western governments never hold bankers to account, but instead bail them out with our money; a clear sign of where the power lies. And while austerity is applied to the lives of the majority, the banking elite not only survive untouched, but increase their wealth so that the gap between rich and poor widens: financial crisis is an opportunity to accumulate assets at a reduced price (just like in the American colonies). With the ability to loan great sums to the government, the Federal Reserve only needed an excuse to make the loans to the US government; and fortunately for them the First World War began in 1914. A further power granted to the Federal Reserve was the right to buy and sell government securities which enabled them to provide loans to other banks. It effectively safe-guarded the Fed from any loss, and as the government entered such huge debt, a means was needed to be able to pay it off. Hence the introduction of income tax, despite it being banned by the constitution: it was accepted by the American people on the assurance that it would never rise above one percent!

Before looking more closely at how the banks operate today, let us pause briefly to consider one more example from history: that of the financial support for both the creation of the NAZIS and the maintenance of the German military during the Second World War. This will give us a clear sense of how disconnected with national concerns the banks are, and how far they place their own profits above our lives.

The Federal Reserve and Bank of England had a long term strategy to take complete control of the economic system of Germany in order to be able to guide the politics of Europe. School children are taught about the reparations demanded of Germany after the First World War, but the real reason for them is never mentioned. After the war, the banks had loaned more than eleven billion dollars (to both sides in the conflict, including the U.S.A.) and in order to pay their debts, the victors decided to force Germany to cover the cost of repayment. The crucial point is, the money was needed to pay back the banks, not to forge a great post-war future. The 1924 Dawes Plan (whose committee chairman was a director of one of the banks in the Morgan group) was formulated in order to stabilise the German Mark in order to benefit American investments. Germany was loaned two hundred million dollars (half of which came from J. P. Morgan) on the basis that American and British banking interests would assume control not only of German repayments, but of the budget and monetary circulation within Germany. The banks had Germany paying them and providing the funds for what was outwardly portrayed as aid: Germany paid its reparations in gold, which was quickly sold off in America, supporting the aid it received which it handed over to Britain and France as reparations, who then repaid America for the war loans they had received. In effect, Germany was reduced to a state of constant debt while the banks accumulated interest on its payments, and the growing wealth of the bankers was funded by a degradation of German living standards. However, by 1929

German industry was booming, but the profits were still being swallowed up by New York banks.

By the 1930s, Rockefeller "Standard Oil" and J. P. Morgan controlled "Interessen-Gemeinschaft Farbenindustine" which provided forty-five percent of Hitler's political campaigns, and subsequently went on to become the main supplier for German military growth. By 1933 Deutsche Bank was completely dependent on American financial capital, and subsequently so was the entire production of German military arms. Perhaps the bankers would claim that they could not have foreseen what was to come, and that they would never have made these investments if they had known what Hitler intended. But in fact in 1941 we find American investment in Germany amounted to four hundred and seventy-five million dollars, of which one hundred and twenty million came from Rockefeller's "Standard Oil" alone. Once more our children are taught half-truths in their history lessons. Neville Chamberlain's choice of appeasement was not just political weakness; he was protecting the interests of American investors. The bankers profit from war, but they do so according to their own schedule and Chamberlain did as was told.

In today's world the banks have grown in size and power. Through The World Bank and International Monetary Fund (IMF) they now exert a level of influence that is unimaginable to most people. The IMF acts like an international loan shark, it exerts disturbing levels of control over more than sixty countries now in its debt. Once a country has accepted an IMF loan it must accept the organisation's demands on how it organises its economy (and spending on health, education, and infrastructure etc.) otherwise it can be refused international assistance and debt relief. The World Bank's assessment of a nation's economic performance determines that country's access to donor aid and investment capital. This makes the IMF one of the most powerful institutions on earth, and yet it has no democratic accountability.

Though technically different organisations, The World Bank and IMF work in tandem and function to achieve the same goals; they are different facets of a single governance system. The World Bank was established in 1946 in order to mobilize funds donated by member governments in order to "assist" struggling nations. It is officially an agency of the United Nations, the difference being that The World Bank provides loans, while the United Nations provides grants. The World Bank is officially owned by a hundred and eighty-five countries, but only eight of them are allowed to have directors on its board: the U.S.A., Japan, the United Kingdom, Germany, France, China, Russia and Saudi Arabia. The board has a chairman who has only ever been American. Unlike other organisations where each country has one vote, voting at The World Bank is weighted according to a country's financial contributions: therefore the wealthiest nations have the loudest voice in the boardroom. A further issue is the level of secrecy under which The World Bank operates: many of its documents are never made public, such as the Country Assistance Strategy, the development plan that guides The World bank's lending to each country.

In recent decades there have been many protests around the world from farmers and various indigenous groups who claim that The World Bank is nothing more than a system of acquiring land and resources at rock bottom prices. The World Bank enforces the "free market" at every opportunity, claiming that the inevitable economic growth that this produces will "trickle down" to those at the bottom of the social and economic pyramid (a philosophy known as neo-liberalism). However, the evidence is to the contrary, we discover The World Bank enforcing a system that benefits the elite economic groups at the expense of the poor. For example, the Swiss Federal Institute of Technology discovered that as a result of The World Bank's activities, there is a group of just a hundred and forty-seven private companies that control over forty percent of corporate wealth in the world. Most of these elite corporations turn out to be western financial groups. Furthermore, recent Wickileaks releases have demonstrated that U.S.

financial organisations have used globalisation as a form of economic colonisation, even using the U.S. State Department to pressure nations on behalf of Monsanto to force them to accept genetically modified crops (the copyrights of which ensure a new form of tax revenue for American corporations).

The mainstream media presents us with terms such as "financial aid" and "foreign direct investment" as though The World Bank and the IMF are living up to their tag line slogan of "Working for a world free of poverty". In reality, these phrases are a smokescreen for what is really happening. Research completed at the London School of Economics demonstrated that for every dollar given in aid, eighteen dollars are taken out by financial institutes and international corporations. In short, this means the flow of money is really only in one direction, from poor countries to rich: it is estimated that the world's poorest countries are losing upwards of two trillion dollars every year, a huge part of which goes to The World Bank. A further lie often repeated by politicians is that by creating wealth, everyone will benefit: Prime Minister Tony Blair famously declared his disinterest in wealth inequality because he believed the poor will be dragged out of poverty as everyone benefits. But this illusion of collective benefit falls apart when we look at the figures: for every dollar of wealth created in the world, ninety-three percent goes to one percent of the world's population: in other words, wealth creation always perpetuates, and even creates, inequality. A further problem is that growing inequality is shown to increase social instability, and so we can see that The World Bank is a cause of social disruption.

One of the chief consequences of all this is pressure on national economies. In poorer countries particularly, we see a cutting of costs whenever possible, which means a fall in social standards, disregard for environmental impacts, and a decrease in wages. This, of course, is no unforeseen accident, but an important element of corporate growth. When politicians are then forced to remove trade barriers and lower corporate taxes, international industries are able to gain access to cheap labour and production costs: when we in the West are able to buy cheap goods, we should remember that the true cost has been paid by those who produce them (and could never hope to purchase them). This reality affects the majority of the world's population: the seventy-nine countries which receive International Development Association funds (forty-one of which are in Sub-Saharan Africa) account for eighty-one percent of people judged to be living in absolute poverty.

There have been many proven cases of projects funded by The World Bank being a direct cause of forced evictions of whole communities and of many abuses of human rights. For example, The Oakland Institute has shown how over twenty thousand people were forced from their land in Uganda as a result of projects financed by The World Bank's International Financial Corporation's funds. The consequence of this kind of displacement in many countries has been the breakdown of local farming methods and the introduction of corporate agricultural methods owned and operated by major international corporations who then profit from the work at the expense of indigenous people. We see this all over the world, from Mali to Guatemala, from Sri Lanka to the Ukraine, and many more. The removal of people's land, income and rights is hidden behind the new terminology used to convince those in the West of the good intentions of the corporations: so we hear of "public-private partnerships" and other misleading phrases which paint a glossy picture over the privatisation of wealth.

It is estimated that twenty-five percent of all World Bank loans are aimed specifically at what is termed "economic reform", which means doing nothing other than bringing local economies into the international free-market. Few indigenous businesses are able to compete with the international corporations when they move in, and governments are prevented by The World Bank from paying any other creditors before servicing their World Bank debt. This means all public services must come second to the repayment to the banks. The effect on the lives of the people supposedly being helped is further worsened by the structure of those debt repayments: for every three dollars received in loans from the International Development Association, two must be repaid directly to The World Bank in debt service.

For a long time those countries which had suffered at the hands of The World Bank and IMF went unheard, and journalists who tried to publicise what is happening were silenced or ridiculed. But in 2002 Joseph Stiglitz, chief economists of The World Bank, was fired because he couldn't remain silent on what he was seeing. He wrote a report that outlined how every country that accepted loans or investments from The World Bank or IMF ended up with a collapsed economy and had its government displaced. Stiglitz revealed how nations' basic assets such as water and power were the real targets of the financial institutions, and that The World Bank forced governments into signing agreements which were known to be so inappropriate for those countries' economies that collapse was inevitable. For example, Enron was able to swoop in and snatch the entire water supply for Buenos Aires at a fraction of its real value, and Stiglitz admitted that the politicians made no attempt to prevent the corruption because they themselves had been paid off with vast sums deposited in Swiss accounts. The game is heavily weighted in the corporations' favour; Lord Wakeham, head of NM Rothschild, was then appointed to the audit committee which gave the thumbs up to Enron's accounts. Interestingly, it was Lord Wakeham who sat in Margaret Thatcher's government and who gave Enron the authorisation to take control over British power plants. Wakeham also has the role of controlling the media's presentation of Enron, which indicates where his loyalties lie.

Stiglitz revealed that The World Bank follows a four point programme. First privatisation is introduced, which permits the nations assets to be stripped. Next the country's capital markets are liberalised to enable money to be easily removed, draining the nation's reserves. The third step is the raising of prices for basic needs such as food, water and power, along with interest rates, on the understanding that the imploding economy needs these responses. This has resulted, for example in fifty-one percent of Ecuadorians being pushed under the poverty line. The consequence of this is often civil unrest, during which further assets may be "protected" by removing capital and investment abroad. The final step in the IMF and World Bank system is what they call a "poverty reduction strategy". Despite the assuring title, this is when the country is forced to accept the World Trade Organisation's rules of business which imposes tariffs and trade laws that are of no benefit to poorer nations, but which protect the interests of the banks.

The IMF maintains publicly that it is not a political organisation, and the mainstream media voices this claim. However, when the Venezuelan government planned to double taxes on international oil companies, the IMF declared that it would give financial support to a transition government if the democratically elected government was removed. The oil revenue was going to be used to support social programmes and the plans were supported by the people: Venezuela is now in serious difficulties.

The foundation for all of this, says Stiglitz, is a World Bank that plots in secret and seeks to carry out its ideology regardless of the economic, social or political consequences. The IMF serves the international financial institutions and creates chaos and enslavement where ever it operates. It forces farmers to shift from food production to cash crops and widespread starvation follows. It prevents governments from providing assistance to its industries while forcing them to compete with heavily subsidised international corporations. It uses tax payers' money to fund itself while providing no opportunity for them to affect its actions.

It is almost impossible to imagine a more corrupt system, and yet this is far from the worst of it. Having established a little of what the bankers have and are doing, let us now see how far they are willing to go in order to establish absolute control over world economics. First we shall consider the extent to which the banks are behind many wars, and how they profit from them. Then we shall consider the links between the banks and some of the themes we have looked at previously, particularly Zionism. Finally we will explore how the bankers intend to use the financial systems to create a form of slavery in which all of us may be captured.

When George W. Bush declared his intention to invade Iraq regardless of whether the United Nations gave him authority to do so, many millions of people questioned his motives. The emotional impact of the attacks which have become known as 9/11 was still being felt across the United States (a country which has never known its cities bombed in war time) and there was a certain amount of confusion. The desire to respond and seek revenge was strong, but who should revenge be met out to? Iraq is and was known to have had nothing whatsoever to do with the attacks, but Tony Blair and others began to repeat Bush's mantra about striking back at terrorism, and a population dazzled by CNN gave its support (although the same pro-war agenda from the BBC was rejected by the majority of UK citizens which resulted in a million protestors taking to the streets of London). Many people began to question what could be the real motivation for invading Iraq; some suggested oil, others that U.S. strategic interests were the issue, but very few people wondered if the answer was the banks. In truth, the reason may have been a combination of factors, but at the head of the list was the plan for total domination by the private central banking system.

The number of Rothschild affiliated central banks around the world is astonishing. They control the finances in the majority of countries, but more telling is the list of countries that have refused their system. In 2000, only seven countries were independent of the Rothschilds: they were Afghanistan, Iraq, Sudan, Libya, Cuba, North Korea and Iran. One glance at this list tells the whole story; it is certainly no coincidence that all of them have been identified by U.S. intelligence as threats to the security of the western world. The plan has been the same from the very beginning: bribe governments into allowing Rothschild banking to take control of the national banking system or face sanctions and/or military invasion. The western public, meanwhile, will have the deaths of foreign civilians and their own serving sons explained as a price worth paying for the downfall of ruthless dictators. Of course, there are many terrible dictators who never enter the picture, such as Robert Mugabe in Zimbabwe, Than Shwe of Burma, King Abdullah of Saudi Arabia, and Gurbanguly Berdymuhammedov of Turkmenistan, for whom CNN and the BBC don't find time to whip up hatred and anger. The demonising of leaders is restricted to those heads of state that persist in protecting their national banks.

The situation has changed since 2000, and we have seen the consequences of this resistance to the Rothschilds. In Afghanistan the state owned banks were viewed by the IMF not to have followed "commonly agreed and accepted standards", which included the refusal by the Taliban to allow banks to charge interest on loans (usury is prohibited in Islam and was punishable by death in some Christian countries in the past). As a result, the banks were no longer lending money at all, and people were turning to a more informal arrangement which could not be monitored or controlled by a central system. Once the U.S. and U.K. had invaded, new banking regulations were immediately put into place and by 2008 almost all banking in Afghanistan had been taken over by western private institutions. As a result, the government there has lost the authority to print and distribute its money and the central banks now act to lend money to the state, thus providing assurance to foreign powers that the government will follow acceptable policies. The Afghanistan people are now paying foreign banks to perform tasks their government should be doing.

Another nation on the list that has been invaded is Iraq (in 2003) of course. It is worth noting that at the time Saddam Hussein took power the country was classed as a "developing nation", but once he had taken the banks into state control, the oil revenues quickly transformed the economy of Iraq. It is not surprising that once the United Nations applied brutal sanctions (that lasted more than a decade) all economic benefits were destroyed. Even as George W. Bush was amassing troops in Kuwait, preparations were under way to put in place a privatised central bank. Within a year of the invasion, the privately owned Central Bank of Iraq (called the Trade Bank of Iraq) was in place, established by none other than J. P. Morgan. The United Nations agreed to allow J. P. Morgan authority to set up banking in Iraq, with all its connections with Rothschild banking.

As we saw in our first chapter, Libya was thriving before Obama and Hillary Clinton decided to invade. But by this point there was little need to hide the true intention, and the creation of a new central bank in Libya began even before the conflict began. Let us remind ourselves of the Libyan condition before the war with an excerpt from a letter sent by a delegation of Russian, Ukrainian and Belarusian doctors settled in Libya to President Vladimir Putin: "They are entitled to free treatment, and their hospitals provide the best in the world of medical treatment. Education is free, capable young people have the opportunity to study abroad at government expense. When marrying, young couples receive sixty thousand Libyan dinars (about fifty thousand dollars) of financial assistance." The Rothschilds would also have known that Libya held more gold bullion as a proportion of gross domestic product than any country except Lebanon (according to the World Gold Council, based in London). When the U.S. led the UN destruction of Libya, almost all of this social and economic benefit was lost: but what did emerge was the Central bank of Libya, based in Benghazi.

Today we see the same process still at work, with all of its appalling consequences. There have been a number of voices crying out about the U.S. attempts to destabilise the government and social structure of Sudan, which includes providing financing the Sudan People's Liberation Army. In Syria the U.S. and U.K. have been giving military and financial aid to Al Qaeda affiliated groups to bring down the Assad government. Former leader of the U.K. Conservative Party William Hague gave numerous speeches in the House of Commons encouraging parliament to support what he called "rebels" in Syria, a country the IMF has for a long time been denouncing for its financial independence. Like Syria, Iran's control over its banking system has, for some time, resulted in U.S. hostility which has gone as far as Senator John McCain calling for direct military action: only support from Russia has so far ensured that Syria and Iran have not faced full scale invasion. Finally, on the list are Cuba and North Korea, both of which attract persistent attention from politicians and media commentators, and both of which have lived with U.S. sanctions for a number of years.

From this we can see that though oil and other factors may have played a part in why the U.S. and U.K. governments have waged war in the Middle East so often over recent decades, the bigger pattern that emerges is the need to establish privately owned central banks under Rothschild control. The Rothschild financial empire is estimated to be worth two hundred and fifty trillion dollars, but more than this, the control over nations through their economies is more valuable. Some economists have suggested that they directly own over half the wealth of the planet, and have influence over most of the other half. Should this worry us? Of course, the centralisation of wealth and power is in itself dangerous, it strips people of real democratic power and leads to slavery. But the fact that the Rothschilds are working to a Zionist agenda is additionally alarming. The Zionists have been prepared to assassinate government leaders and stir people to revolution, but there is something more that we must recognise: Zionism is intensely anti-Christian. To support this charge we will focus later on examples of direct attacks made against the Church and traditional Christian values. Before we examine exactly how this monopoly of central banks is intended to establish slavery of all humanity, let us just consider what has happened to Greece.

In September 1974 U.S. Secretary of State Henry Kissinger made a speech which was later quoted in the Greek magazine "Oikonomikos Tachydromos" He said:

"The Greek people are anarchic and difficult to tame. For this reason we must strike deep into their cultural roots: Perhaps then we can force them to conform. I mean, of course, to strike at their language, their religion, their cultural and historical reserves, so that we can neutralise their ability to develop, to distinguish themselves, or to prevail, thereby removing them as an obstacle to our strategically vital plans in the Balkans, the Mediterranean, and the Middle East."

Kissinger later denied saying these things, but the quotation has been widely circulated as representing the Zionist attitude towards this Orthodox Christian nation. It is no surprise that when Turkish paratroopers invaded Cyprus the United Nations looked away and many Greek Cypriots had their land, homes and churches stolen, never to be returned. Henry Kissinger worked hard to have lifted the arms embargo imposed on Turkey, claiming that otherwise Turkey would likely look to other Muslim nations in the Middle East as allies rather than to western powers, which would threaten the security of Israel. Kissinger argued that the Jewish lobbyists should be made aware of this to bring pressure on the U.S. administration over the issue of Cyprus. CIA documents released since then have proved Kissinger's involvement in Turkey's invasion of Cyprus. U.N. documents from this time reveal that Washington considered Greece a problem long before this because of the Greek government's desire to withdraw from America's "cold war" with the U.S.S.R.. Western powers saw Greece as nothing more than a small piece in the larger game it was playing, and as early as 1967 the CIA had been planning to impose the Papadopoulos regime on Greece: the coup that resulted was heavily populated by men who had close links with the CIA. But behind it all was Kissinger's principle concern: the protection of the Jewish state in Israel at any cost.

The Greek financial crisis must be seen in the context of this longer history, because only in this way can we understand the real motives for the way Greece has been treated. Few of us living in other countries were aware of how relentless the attacks on the Greek people were in the German media. Greeks were portrayed as a lazy, untrustworthy nation who were seeking debt forgiveness because of their selfish lifestyle. Of course, the German people seemed to have forgotten how they themselves were the beneficiary of the greatest debt forgiveness in the history of the world. In 1948, U.S. banks removed Germany's domestic debt by financing the new Deutsche Mark. And again, in 1953, half of Germany's external debts were removed in order to allow the recovery of the German economy: this at a time when Germany's debt only accounted for twenty percent of its GDP while some other European countries at the time were facing debts worth up to two hundred percent of their GDP. The plain truth is that after German forces had run amok across Europe, their economy was then granted three times more debt forgiveness than was needed by Greece in 2010. And the Greek request to pay off its debt from its economic surplus (a request that was rejected) was exactly the same as the conditions granted to Germany in 1953. Greece has been portrayed in the European media and by the EU's politicians as bringing on itself its own destruction, but this is completely untrue: for decades German bankers lent ridiculous amounts of money to one corrupt Greek government after another, and the Rothschild owned Goldman Sachs deliberately hid the true depth of the Greek debt when Greece was being drawn into the euro.

The whole Greek economic crisis has been orchestrated for one purpose: to protect private European banks, particularly those of France and Germany. This is born out in two IMF previously secret documents which have been publicised by the Truth Committee on Greek Public Debt (documents dated from February to October 2015). The documents reveal that the IMF could have solved the Greek financial problem but that this would have required the private banks to have contributed. In order to avoid this, the German and French directors of the IMF misled everyone by giving the assurance that their banks would hold on to Greek bonds. Subsequently the banks sold off the bonds, which had two direct effects: it weakened the Greek economy further and it transferred the financial liability from themselves to European tax payers. Any reduction of Greek debt would have required the Greek bankers to contribute to the rescue package, which they were unwilling to do. Since Greece was tied in to the Euro, it could not devalue its currency, as would be normal in this situation, and so the only solution permitted was to reduce Greek wages, pensions, and the government's social spending. At the same time international financiers swooped in and began stripping the country of its assets. Consequently the European private banks were protected, the bailout was focussed on achieving this, while the Greek people face spiralling debt: from 2009 to 2011, Greek debt rose from two hundred and ninety-nine billion euros to three hundred and fifty-five billion, a hike of nearly nineteen percent. None of the IMF forecasts for the Greek recovery have proven correct, and generations of Greeks are facing hardship that has resulted directly from the

IMF's policies. Henry Kissinger's hopes for a devastated Greece have finally been achieved through the work of the banks.

The story of Greece is typical of many countries; it demonstrates the bankers' objectives very clearly. But there is an even more disturbing agenda within the banking system that threatens us all: the removal of physical money so that we are made dependent on digital financing. To understand why this is a threat, let us first see the true nature of money. Most people imagine that banks lend out money which has been previously deposited by other customers; so that when we take out a loan, we are borrowing money earned and created by someone else's work. But in reality this is not the case. When banks make loans, they are creating the money which is handed out. The loans are really an IOU, and so long as they can find someone to borrow it, the banks can keep producing money. Few of us receive major loans in cash, the imaginary numbers are lent to us and we then deposit the sum back into the bank. In this way, every loan is turned into a deposit, and while governments carry out fiscal easing, that is, printing more money, with zero interest rates, the limit to how much money they can produce is not based on inflation or any factor other than how much governments and ordinary people are willing to borrow. Most of us spend our lives working to pay off a mortgage that never existed as hard currency, but was brought into existence by the bank when it loaned it to us. Governments are pretending to get tough with banks, and insisting that a certain reserve must be held to cover a percentage of these loans, but this is another sleight of hand, the banks continue to create money.

But even if this was the limit to the problem, things would not be too bad. Most of us would be happy to work and finally own our own home and hope to pass on a little wealth to our children. But if the banks introduced negative interest, we would all withdraw our money, there would be a run on the banks, but we would still have our cash under the bed. The aim is to remove all physical cash to prevent us from doing this. The switch to an electronic currency will be the basis for total control over us. There is evidence to support the claim that the introduction of the euro was never an end in itself, but a means of removing many national currencies as a first step to electronic money. We see an encouragement by banks and retailers to use electronic means of payment, and we are being assured of the ease and security of this new form of transaction. A future financial crisis may be created in order to convince us that part of the solution will be electronic finance, or else people may be persuaded to throw away their control by voluntarily switching because it is portrayed as yet another great technological advance. In April 2016 BBC Radio 4 was running a nightly series of articles questioning the value and purpose of retaining cash: establishing the issue in people's minds to make it easier once the banks make their move.

Electronic currency means governments will follow every exchange that takes place: none of us will be able to buy anything without it being recorded; we will lose any right to anonymity and this level of monitoring has always proved to be a threat to freedom. Our personal wealth will be known moment by moment, and it would be possible to refuse us the right to spend our money as we see fit if it went against government policy. It would be equally simple for governments to fine us for what they consider inappropriate activities or even wipe our entire savings from the system as a form of punishment. Any dissent will be impossible if we wish to buy food or pay rent, and dissent may include holding certain religious beliefs. And of course, so long as we use cash the banks cannot take a cut when we buy something: with an electronic currency charges and taxes can be applied to everything we do.

Electronic currency also makes it more possible to introduce a single world currency, since distinctive notes and coins will have been removed. Such a world currency will enable banks to gain absolute control over the flow of money, and it will no longer be just the transactions of individuals under their control, but whole nations and governments. We have already begun to see the end of physical currency, in Sweden for example and also the Chase bank has announced that it will no longer accept cash deposits from non-account holders. Currency exchange dealers are now offering cards instead of hard currency, always on the basis that it is for our benefit. We are already much further along the road to this single world governance than most of us dare admit. So long as we can withdraw our money we can rein in the activities of the banks, but once we reach a cashless society we will be enslaved. It is being argued by the European bank and the IMF that there should be a limit imposed on Greece as to how much currency it should be permitted, so that full control can be maintained to ensure their debts are paid before all else. Negative interest rates will be with us soon, introduced through charges made for depositing cash and no doubt extended to all use of physical money. John Cryan, CEO of Deutsche Bank has predicted that physical cash will have disappeared by 2025.

Control of a nation's currency is the real source of power over a people: and a power they often will not understand is being exercised. So long as people remain in debt they are not free to risk their jobs or homes by protesting what is happening. The promise of financial freedom is forever dangled before them, and though they may work hard, the majority will not achieve it. And governments will no longer be able to make provision for the sick or elderly when the system is rigged in favour of the private banks. The private banks are extending their monopoly to encompass the whole world, and clearly, those who stand in their way are being removed through military force. Banking is more profitable than any other kind of business, but is also the true source of power in the world.

But the banks have not yet achieved their goal, and we must not lose hope. Following the financial crash of 2008, the Icelandic people recognised what was happening, and unlike any other European nation, held the bankers responsible. In the U.K. and elsewhere bankers continued to award themselves handsome bonuses and increase the gap between themselves and the people paying for their actions. Meanwhile, In Iceland, the banks' claims that they "were too big to fail" was ignored, they were allowed to go bust, and many of the bankers themselves were tried and imprisoned. So long as we remain ignorant of their systems we will be victims to their corruption. What we are witnessing is a centralisation of power that has been anticipated for two thousand years. Christians should not be surprised by what is happening, but nor should we be afraid of naming it: a move to one world government.

Chapter 10 ~ One World Government

As we begin to tie these themes together we see an organised plan to coordinate a wide variety of organisations so that finance and power is placed in the hands of a tiny elite group. This centralisation of influence and control is presented as a solution to world problems; it is promoted with the false language of utopian idealism. The ultimate goal is a single world government, an idea supported by a variety of people who give the impression that they speak with different motives and loyalties, but in fact are united in a single cause. To some readers this may sound an alarmist set of claims, in fact most ordinary people might imagine it as nothing more than a conspiracy theory. So let us look at the evidence, and recognise that this is not a fantasy or over-heated interpretation, but the stated intention of the elite for many decades.

It was only five years after the end of the Second World War that Winston Churchill made a speech in Copenhagen where he stated: "Unless some effective world supergovernment can be brought quickly into action, the proposals for peace and human progress are dark and doubtful." This is the classic approach used many times, the claim that individual nations governed to meet their own needs must be overcome if we are to avoid further war. Most people want peace, and so our natural desire is manipulated to suggest that anyone opposing the establishment of this "supergovernment" is somehow rejecting peace. The latest terminology includes "internationalism" and "globalism", each with their particular inference of positive, outward looking attitudes to others.

Immediately after the war, Bertrand Russell wrote extensively on the need for a world government, for example in his book "Has Man a Future?" Russell promoted what became known as the Baruch Plan (after Bernard Baruch) which was presented to government leaders including Churchill and Stalin. It was only Stalin's fear that such a plan would give too much power to Washington that led him to reject it. But worthy of note is the fact that Baruch was a Zionist Jew, and with his fellow Zionist David Lilienthal, he managed to gain a great deal of support amongst other Zionist scientists working on the Manhattan Project (including Father of the Atom bomb" Robert Oppenheimer) for the establishment of a single world government (Lilienthal and Baruch edited the "Bulletin of Atomic Scientists"). Baruch went on to become an adviser for five different U.S. presidents and continued to argue for a one world government. He was able to find support from the scientific community because many of the displaced Jews working in America on the atomic weapons programme were not loyal to either side in the Cold War, but to what they considered a set of universal principles that transcended national loyalties. The great irony in all this is that by creating the atom bomb they were able to argue that the danger their invention posed required a single world government to overcome its threat. Baruch repeatedly called for the abolition of the permanent members of the UN Security Council having a veto in the decision-making process. Baruch's arguments gained a great deal of support from the bankers of his day, just as they continue to support the call for one world government today.

There were others who recognised what was being done, and while some spoke out to encourage the plan, others tried to warn the general population of where they were being led. For example, in February of 1950, James Paul Warburg (whose father Paul Warburg had been the author of the Federal Reserve Act) said: "We shall have World Government, whether or not we like it. The only question is whether World Government will be achieved by consent or conquest."

The strategy is very simple; it is the destruction of national, democratic governments by removing their power, law by law. As former U.S. Deputy Assistant Secretary Richard Gardner said "a run around national sovereignty, eroding it piece by piece, will accomplish much more than the old-fashioned frontal assault."

And again, U.S. Senator William Jenner in 1954 said: "Today the path of total dictatorship in the United States can be laid by strictly legal means, unseen and unheard by the Congress, the President, or the people. Outwardly we have a constitutional government. We have operating within our government and political system, another body representing another form of government – bureaucratic elite." Today many people have begun to refer to this as the "dark government" it is a reality that most political observers are aware of but not something the mainstream media dares to reveal to the public.

At the centre of this elite we find the Rockefeller organisation (it is no longer simply a family), and from his memoirs we read David Rockefeller's own admission that these claims are true. He writes: "Some even believe we are a part of a secret cabal working against the best interests of the United States, characterising my family and me as "internationalists" and of conspiring with others around the world to build a more integrated global political and economic structure – one world, if you will. If that's the charge, I stand guilty and I am proud of it."

In fact the plan has been in existence for centuries, as we shall see, it has been the long term goal of Freemasons for hundreds of years.

Benjamin Disraeli (the first Jewish British Prime Minister) wrote in "The New Generation": "The world is governed by very different personages from what is imagined by those who are not behind the scenes." He also wrote: "The governments of the present day have to deal not merely with other governments, with emperors, kings and ministers, but also with the secret societies which have everywhere their unscrupulous agents, and can at the last moment, upset all the government's plans."

Disraeli's observation of the real nature of power in Britain was confirmed by Felix Frankfurter (U.S. Supreme Court Justice) as being exactly the same in the U.S.A. when, in 1952 he said "The real rulers in Washington are invisible, and exercise power from behind the scenes." The formation of a single world government requires this alternative control since democratic governments are too dependent on the will of the people. Power that is invisible and unaccountable is also transferable, and can be exercised from anywhere in the world. It can also be exercised over many, if not all nations. How many times we here the BBC and other mainstream media repeat their mantra of "western democracy" and "the birthplace of democratic government"; the lie is repeated often enough to become reality in the minds of the general population. And should someone question these notions, mainstream journalists can always point and compare Britain with places where tyrants are so brutal and so open about their oppressive intentions that the objector is made to look foolish.

Finally, we hear these plans articulated by President Clinton's Deputy Secretary of State, Strobe Talbot, who stated in a July 1992 interview in Time "In the next century, nations as we know it will be obsolete; all states will recognise a single, global authority. National sovereignty wasn't such a great idea after all."

The situation today is that the plan for One World Government has never been closer to being a reality. Each year we see a variety of organisations like the United nations, The World Bank, The European Bank, the European Union, the International Monetary Fund, the Nuclear Energy Agency, The International Chamber of Commerce and many others creating further treaties and international agreements that act to centralise further the governance of individual nations. All this takes place without agreement from the people; there is no requirement for any kind of democratic mandate when the decision makers themselves have no accountability to the electorate. Let us look a little closer at some of these new agreements, how they are portrayed by the mainstream media, and where they are taking us.

The UN has launched what it calls in its own core document, a "new universal agenda" for humanity. Seventeen goals were established, signed off by almost every nation on earth and backed by the presence of Pope Francis who stated that "The adoption of the 2030 Agenda for Sustainable Development is an important sign of hope." Despite the enormity of the event and the high level agreement it was met with, there was little mention of it in our news bulletins. In effect, the UN has prescribed a programme of "sustainability" which it has called the "2030 Plan". Much of its content covers the same ground as Agenda 21, but this time the focus is in establishing a global economic system in order to achieve "fairness" and "justice". The agenda was promoted separately by an event called the "Global Citizen Festival" in Central Park, where young people were entertained by the likes of Beyonce. The message was very clear, young people are to see themselves as "global citizens", part of a "global community". Of course, decent people will understand this to mean showing concern for every person on the planet, and seeking a fairer share of resources and opportunities for everyone. This is the way the new language portrays the plan. But the reality is that as we lose control over our nation states, the international banking families exert their power to suit themselves. History shows us that they have been willing to sacrifice millions of lives in war to achieve their goals: if we think for a moment that these elites are concerned with the wellbeing of the rest of us we are living with our heads in the sand.

The power elites intend to create a single world market that operates according to their rules and conditions. We already see major companies like Dyson moving its production from the United Kingdom to harvest the wealth of cheap labour in Asia. The infamous Trans-Pacific Partnership that President Obama was working to establish would control forty percent of the entire world's economy, and would enable, for example, U.S. companies to refuse to label genetically modified crops in their products (since European consumers do not want to eat them) and no one would be able to force them to do so. It would also allow U.S. corporations to sue European governments if they feel their ability to trade is being inhibited while denying governments the right to sue the companies. In other words, the organisations supposedly representing the people, governments, would be less powerful than the international corporations concerned only with making a profit.

In 1995, the UN Commission on Global Governance recommended that the UN be restructured to include a system of global taxation, an international criminal court (which was established in 1998), the formation of a world parliament and the creation of a standing UN army. We are led to believe that humanity is threatened by various crises, and only international experts and scientists are able to save us. The world's problems need a united solution: but the UN is really an international banking system which was established by, and to serve the needs of an elite few. The goal is to reduce our rights and ability to protest, and as we become enslaved by debt, transform us into commercial units. But this can only be achieved by breaking down the existing order of governance and social structure. To achieve this there needs to be chaos, crises, fear and impending disaster. People need to feel so insecure that they look to the powerful for protection, even being willing to give away their basic rights in order to remain safe. As Henry Kissinger said (in Evians, France, in 1991): "Today, America would be outraged if UN troops entered Los Angeles to restore order. Tomorrow they will be grateful. This is especially true if they were told that there were an outside threat from beyond, whether real or promulgated, that threatened our very existence. It is then that all peoples of the world will plead to be delivered from evil. The one thing that every man fears is the unknown. When presented with this scenario, individual rights will be willingly relinquished for the guarantee of their well-being granted to them by the World Government." Just as David Rockefeller said: "We are on the verge of a global transformation. All we need is the right major crisis and the nations will accept the New World order."

Plans for this international army go beyond the present blue helmets. The UN intends to have a permanent military that can be used independently of any national concerns: eliminating national sovereignty completely. UN Secretary General Kofi Annan expressed this intention when he said "A world government can intervene militarily in the affairs of any nation when it disapproves of their activities." Therefore, even if a government is acting according to its people's wishes, Annan foresees a time when the supreme world government will be able to act according to its own agenda and override national interests. George Bush (senior) believed too that this was the right path for humanity to follow. In a speech made in 1992 he said "It is the sacred principles enshrined in the United Nations charter to which the American people will henceforth pledge their allegiance." These statements do not belong to a distant future, but are already in our past.

We are being convinced as part of the programme that our continued existence is under threat. It was once the idea that nuclear weapons would be launched from the U.S.S.R., for a while we were being told it was "global warming" (a term they have stopped using in favour of "climate change") and alongside environmental disaster there is the endless war on terror. We are being trained to accept an existential threat, something that we instinctively must react against. Just like those American patriots who supported the invasion of Iraq, because something had to be done after

"9/11", even if what was being done had nothing to do with the event. All of this was recognised by John Paul II who wrote: "By the end of this decade we will live under the first One World Government that has ever existed…a government with absolute authority to decide the basic issues of survival. One World Government is inevitable." He expected things to move more quickly than they have, but he was promoting the same agenda of a single world government in order to protect us.

These statements point to a disturbing reality, they create a weight of evidence that points to the one world government agenda that is difficult to refute. But accepting that the plan is real is one thing, understanding the secret groups which orchestrate it requires other evidence. We have seen that many high level decision makers over the last few hundred years have been Freemasons, but let us add to that list more contemporary figures such as Henry Kissinger, Dick Chaney, Colin Powell, Al Gore, Ariel Sharon, World bank president James Wolfensohn, and many others. We have seen that the only space provided for worship in the UN was designed and is maintained by Satanists belonging to the Lucis Trust. At the heart of the planned new world order is a pagan religion that through its pretence of tolerating all religions intends to suppress authentic Christianity. We shall see in our next chapter how the UN promotes false ideas of liberation and freedom that amount to uncontrolled sexual activity and a distortion of human consciousness. Christian sensibilities are under attack, and we shall examine this in more detail later as part of our examination of how we are being manipulated, but for now, let us look at how Freemasons have grown so confident that they display their encroaching victory for all to see.

On 9th September 2001, the Twin Towers were destroyed. In their place has been built the "One World Trade Centre"; the name itself speaks of a global agenda. Before the building was erected, designers Kristin Jones and Andrew Ginzel had occult symbols built into the World Trade Centre subway stop beneath the site. The designers call their work "Oculus", meaning eye, and it is made up of three hundred mosaic eyes placed around the station and various parts of the site. The all-seeing eye of Horus was named by Albert Pike as representing the all-seeing eye of Lucifer, and its presence indicates to others in the know of the allegiance of those who placed them there. It is openly acknowledged by the architects that the new Trade Centre building is based on the Washington Monument, patterned after Nebukadnezzar's obelisk which, in pagan cults, represents a phallus. The outer surface of the building is designed to look like an Egyptian pyramid, and like in the subway station, there are many tiles on its interior walls depicting the all-seeing eye. The building is one thousand, seven hundred and seventy-six feet tall, marking the year 1776 in which the U.S. Declaration of Independence was signed.

The entire building is designed to communicate occult power, it symbioses Masonic authority, not just in the U.S., but as the name of the building suggests, over the whole world. On the U.S. dollar bill we find the Latin words "E Pluribus Unem" which means "Order out of chaos". The fall of the Twin Towers was an emotional as well as national moment of chaos for many people, and in their place there now stands a monument to the true power of this world.

But for Orthodox Christians there is a clearer perspective on all of this. We read the events through the eyes of faith, and recognise the work of evil. We know that Satan persists in imitating God, producing counterfeit substitutes for God's truth. We see how yoga teachers promise inner peace, how Hindu gurus perform illusions claiming them to be miracles, how the atheistic communists placed Lenin's body for permanent veneration like some incorruptible saint: and finally Satan's mockery will extend to sending a false messiah who will claim to be Christ. In preparation he has a counterfeit Israel, not the people of God (the Church) but a Zionist body brought about through tanks and rockets. And who is it who rejects God's messiah and still waits for him to come? Who then will welcome the Antichrist, since they alone still live in expectation of his coming? It is in Jerusalem that Antichrist will establish his reign over the earth, but first there will be more chaos. Already we see biblical prophecy coming to pass, the kings of the world are already under the control of a greater power, the beginnings of world government, and it is through this all-powerful organisation that the Antichrist will dominate all nations. In the ancient mystery cults and Kabbalistic teachings, passed on through the secret societies, the synagogue of Satan has perpetuated its works in darkness, from Babylon and Egypt the evil teachings have now manifest their intentions in our modern world. We are distracted, our senses are being blunted, we have the illusion of being able to change political leaders who carry with them the stigma of all they have done while untainted, fresh leaders take their place, and we are told that things will improve.. Meanwhile the secret cults operate their banking systems, pass laws that slowly strip us of our independence and dignity, working towards their new world order of totalitarian power and economic slavery. But let us be clear, even when one world government is established, we have not yet reached the end, for the man of iniquity is still to come to take his crown.

Our task now is to examine how we are being prepared for all of this. It is not enough that we become economic slaves, since even slaves can hold firm to their faith. In order for Antichrist to be welcomed and worshipped, Christian faith must be attacked. In the remaining chapters we shall look at how the law, social attitudes, religious belief and human psychology are being manipulated to degrade our capacity to reject evil. Cultural norms are changing more quickly than ever before. The new language is becoming an oppressive tool that is already enabling the good to be named as bad and evil to be named as good. This acceleration of the agenda is infecting every aspect of our lives, and as we shall see, there have been many holy saints who were given insight into what is happening, and how we must protect ourselves.

Chapter 11 ~ Education

If a single world government is to achieve power it must reduce the average man to a condition where he is more easily controlled, more easily led. As J. D. Rockefeller once said "I don't want a nation of thinkers. I want a nation of workers." In order for this to be achieved the nature of education had to, and is being changed. After teaching for fourteen years in U.K. state secondary schools I witnessed for myself many of the examples of change that this chapter will outline. At the time I scratched my head in bewilderment, and in private conversation with other teachers found I was not the only one to see how far the methods and philosophy of modern education are moving away from what the professionals know to be common sense. After identifying some of these changes, we shall look at where they come from, the agenda behind them, and finally how our schools are becoming the new front line in the battle being waged against authentic Christianity.

One of the key aims of the new agenda for education is to limit access to knowledge. Someone who knows about history, geography, science, how to use statistics etc. is more able to protect themselves from false ideas and manipulation. Teachers are now required to demonstrate their teaching at least once each term to someone in their management, and if they are considered unsatisfactory in any two observations they will be placed on what is called "competency": in other words they may be sacked. It was a common complaint amongst my colleagues that normal teaching would have to be put on hold while a special lesson was demonstrated, something which would often take a number of hours to prepare (and so was not something that could be done regularly as part of usual teaching). But the real problem for teachers was that to achieve a good observation level, the lesson would have to include group and class discussions which would result in the class group falling behind other groups in their progress. In other words, to teach the way management are now expecting from staff, the teaching of subjects would be slowed or even completely put on pause, while the students participated in the activities now considered good learning.

This has a number of dangers. The first problem is that lessons now considered successful are those where the teacher talks very little. Despite the students having something of an expert in the particular subject there in the classroom, that person is not permitted to impart knowledge to the class. Teaching today is not about content, but methodology. Students must learn from one another in groups, but since none of them has the knowledge to impart to the rest of the group, learning remains superficial and empty of real detail. It is supposed to engender a "cooperative" approach to learning, but in reality it ensures that even bright children will be inhibited in their learning by the level of progress of the slowest learner in the group. And groups are arranged so that high and lower lever students work together in order to benefit the less able. The traditional idea of a teacher as a source of information which the child is able to learn and digest is unacceptable in U.K. state schools: instead the teacher facilitates the child's learning. But the state continues to identify failing schools and blames bad teachers, while all the time insisting that all teachers adopt the one-size-fits-all approach to teaching which creates days in school for students which have become repetitive and tedious. I was once criticised in a lesson observation for expecting students to use a text book: the observer questioned why I hadn't used a power point like other staff. And these schools labelled as failing are now quickly placed in the control of private corporations, where the agenda for removing traditional Christianity is even more intensely pursued.

Students in state schools are now experiencing more standardised testing than at any other time: and since the teachers' careers and the schools' reputations are judged on the basis of the results of these tests, is it any wonder that education is now focussed so completely on teaching to the tests? President Clinton's Goals 2000 Act ensured that the U.S. government could by-pass local interests by making federal funds available on the basis of performance in these tests. This kind of testing and teaching does nothing for the individual child, it doesn't cultivate their particular skills, it doesn't encourage their interests, and the children are constantly reminded that their performance in these tests will determine the likelihood of their future success in life. Motivation to work is turned into a threat of financial and social poverty if they do not work to the tests. Education is being reduced to an opportunity to acquire job skills, while at the same time deskilling teachers. After I had been teaching for about ten years I was talking to a friend who had worked for a similar period of time as a social worker. He mentioned how good it felt to have worked long enough to become confident in his profession, and even to be able to advise newer staff. I told him that the opposite is true in teaching, that with each new wave of innovations and educational theories, teachers were constantly finding the expectations of what constitutes good teaching changing, and so older staff were often perceived as out of date or struggling to incorporate the latest ideas. As a result, many experienced, older staff are leaving the teaching profession, and it is not uncommon to enter a school's staff room to find almost everyone under the age of forty.

My friend's response was to suggest that if the educationalists were constantly changing the approach to teaching, it must be because they do not really know what will work. But this naïve interpretation of events misses the reality of what is taking place: a deliberate guiding of students into an occult perception of life that has its roots in the teachings of Alice Bailey, and which is being forced into educational systems around the world by the UN.

The United Nation's Educational, Scientific, and Cultural Organisation (UNESCO) grew out of the Rockefeller-funded International Bureau of Education. It has established an International Baccalaureate that is now being taught in over a hundred and forty countries, but few citizens of those places will have had a say in this or even be aware that it exists. Its aim is to promote a global education agenda in order to change a whole generation's attitudes and perception of itself.

On UNESCO's Global Citizenship Webpage we read "Global Citizenship Education is one of the strategic areas of work for UNESCO's education programme and one of the three priorities of the UN Secretary General's Global Education First Initiative launched in September 2012." The webpage goes on to use the familiar buzzwords of justice and equality, but at the heart of the message is the concept of "diversity". This is a word school children hear repeatedly; to become citizens of the whole planet they must embrace every kind of belief and lifestyle as being equally valid.

However, this is a particularly strange kind of tolerance, since students who proclaim belief in objective, revealed truth are quickly challenged, since the true nature of tolerance is not respect for different beliefs, but the insistence on moral relativism. The neo-liberalism espoused in state schools today is tolerance for anything that does not disagree with this empty relativism. As long as no one believes that what they have been taught by their parents and church community is actually objectively true, then they will be tolerated. The emphasis on group work and problem solving is aimed at inducing doubt and uncertainty, and only through inquiry along carefully controlled parameters is the student able to resolve their doubt: if a student enters this kind of activity with pre-existing beliefs then he cannot participate fully in the kind of problem solving the lesson demands. The intention is to transform students' "unexamined beliefs" into problems to be tackled and solved, and this is absolutely necessary if children are to accept the new agenda, since they will be reluctant to go along with it if they believe it is wrong. Many of these ideas come from the work of John Dewey, who is often given the title "the father of progressive education". Dewey argued that thinking is a collective rather than individual phenomena, and that students should be taught social values rather than academic skills: he claimed that social progress is only possible when we overcome the individual mind in favour of the group.

A further aspect of this is the necessity to drive a wedge between children and their parents: it is no accident that teenagers today are often observed to experience more of an emotional distance from their parents than ever before. The types of activities students are required to participate in manipulate them into an emotional response so that they become involved on some level: children's sense of empathy is deliberately invoked (in fact it is listed as one of the key skills that U.K. education must develop). Children find themselves guided into an emotional response that will be at odds with the teaching of their parents and church and so must inevitably see their parents' attitudes as just one more voice to be considered amongst many (in a world where the voice of the teacher is presented as the one of professional, rational judgement). The process further wastes students' time while they are forced to listen to the uniformed opinions of their classmates, and do so in an atmosphere where they have been taught that all beliefs and attitudes must be respected and listened to. I have witnessed situations where Christian children have had to sit and listen to a Jehovah's Witness member repeat his parents' dogma and the teacher has been unable to confront the true nature of this cult since the school requires all students' "cultural identities" to be treated equally.

So let us examine how the UN is at work in all of this, and why they are pursuing this agenda. In the U.S.A. some parents have been alerted to what is called the Common Core curriculum, which is promoted as coming from local educators but in reality is funded and driven by the global aim for education. Common Core is taken from the World Core Curriculum, created by Robert Muller (former UN Assistant Secretary General), who wrote a number of New Age books such as "New Genesis: Shaping A Global Spirituality". In his books Muller expressed his longing for the United Nations to establish a single world government; something he believed was an inevitability because divine forces are supporting it. In "My Testament" he writes: "The divine success and supreme progress of the United Nations is bound to become a reality. At this choice hour, the Absolute Supreme will ring his own victory-bell here on Earth through the loving and serving heart of the United Nations." This is not some obscure, New Age guru saying this, but the one-time Assistant Secretary General of the UN. Common Core is a subsidiary of Core International which turns out to be an information technology company which is officially a publicly traded company – though only to be found on the Indian Stock Exchange. Without any media attention, Core International has had a growth rate of fifty-two percent over the last five years, making it the fastest growing company in

196

India. President Obama made funding of his educational programme "Race To The Top" dependent on schools accepting the Common Core curriculum. We should not be surprised to learn that Common Core is also a key element of the UN's Agenda 21.

In his drive to achieve one world government, Muller recognised how vital a role education must play in it, particularly in overcoming the teachings of Christianity. In "New Genesis" he wrote: "We must outgrow the increasingly erroneous notion of good and bad as seen by a particular group, and define new concepts of what is good and bad for the entire human family. This is absolutely essential." It is not surprising that we now see this philosophy at work in our state schools since he occupied his post in the UN for over forty years. Muller was awarded the UNESCO Prize for Peace Education in 1989, and managed to have the LGBT and pro-abortion agenda adopted into many nations' educational curriculum, including the U.K. and the U.S.A. This has been achieved by promoting an education which is rights-based, that individual choice over moral questions is absolute, and that there can never be shared, objective moral values when it comes to sexual behaviour or abortion (other than the one of moral relativism, of course).

Robert Muller established a group of schools which were based on the teachings of Alice Bailey.

In the Robert Muller World Core Curriculum it states: "The underlying philosophy upon which the Robert Muller School is based will be found in the teaching set forth in the books of Alice Bailey." This has now become the basis for curriculum in many states across America as well as countries in Europe, and was Muller's tool for establishing the UN global project. Bailey herself wrote in her book "Education in the New Age" that children should be introduced to astrology, meditation, and various pagan beliefs such as oneness with nature and reincarnation. We must remember that Bailey received her writings from her spirit guide Djwhal Khul: it is the beliefs of the Lucifer Trust that are now the basis for much of our public education in the West.

The Rockefeller Foundation has been a powerful force in the shaping of education, particularly in America, with a very particular plan for American children. The first mission statement of the Rockefeller-funded General Education board stated in 1906: "We shall not try to make these people or any of their children into men of learning or philosophers, or men of science. We have not to raise up from them authors, educators, poets or men of letters, artists, musicians, lawyers, doctors, statesmen or politicians, creatures of whom we have ample supply. The task is simple. We will organise children and teach them in a perfect way the things their fathers and mothers are doing in an imperfect way." J. D. Rockefeller created the General Education Board in 1905 with huge sums of money, and by 1950 the Foundation's-endowed Columbia Teacher College was producing one third of all the men who went on to become the presidents of American teacher training colleges, as well as a fifth of all teachers.

It is not only the personnel that are Rockefeller owned, the Foundation controls many of the companies producing educational text books, giving them direct control over the history taught to American citizens. One example of how this power is exerted is the story of the automobile. In the early 1900s Henry Ford had designed his cars capable of switching from petrol to alcohol as a fuel. Rockefeller Standard Oil did not want car owners to be able to purchase alcohol which could be produced by any farmer at the side of the road, and so they engineered what became prohibition. Ford switched to petrol, while movies and school text books recorded prohibition as being a social issue rather than a business move. The Rockefeller text books had sold more than five million copies into teacher training colleges by 1940, including "The Great Technology" which opens with the words: "Education must be used to condition the people to accept social change. The chief function of schools is to plan the future of society."

Rockefeller and Carnegie sought to implement their plan by taking control of U.S. schools district by district. However, after moving on to New York, the man assigned to supervise the programme in 1917, William Wirt, realised what was happening and tried to warn the public. He began making speeches about the plot to use the educational system to enable an elite to take control of America: Wirt was committed to an insane asylum.

The agenda was also recognised for what it was in 1952 by U.S. Senator William Jenners who became alarmed at the level of influence the Rockefeller organisations were having in American education. He is recorded in the congressional records as saying: "The UN is at work every day and night, changing the teachers, changing the teaching materials, changing the very words and tones – changing all the essential ideas which we imagine our schools are teaching our young folk." Sadly, we could repeat these sentiments today, but we are now nearly sixty years further along in the plan.

Anyone who has undergone teacher training in the last thirty years will be familiar with Bloom's "Taxonomy of Educational Objectives". In the U.K. today teachers are required to incorporate Bloom's terminology into their lesson objectives, but few are given the full picture of Dr. Bloom's philosophy. Bloom saw education as being the means to creating workers more suitable for a successful economy. He also argued for education to be used as a means of controlling children's opinions, and the approach now used in our schools is based on the belief that it is possible to design education that allows us to classify and grade children's thoughts and feelings when participating in class activities. Let us be clear, the objective is not to assess whether children have gained knowledge and understanding, but that they are engaging with particular attitudes.

One of the key areas of the new educational agenda is sex education. When I first started teaching it was explicitly stated in government materials that teachers were to promote abstinence amongst children and that all other information was to be presented from this perspective. Within ten years I saw this approach completely abandoned, but I had no idea that at the heart of the UN's program was the promotion of the understanding that we are all to perceive ourselves as agents making free choices independently of external moralities; sexual desire is therefore to be seen as one way of expressing ourselves and finding fulfilment. Sex education in schools now focuses on the use of condoms and the insistence that all forms of sexual "expression" are to be viewed as equal and legitimate. In all U.K. state schools children have access to contraception without their parents' knowledge or consent; this includes the so-called morning-after pill which is a chemical destruction of a foetus that may have been conceived. Abortion is taught as an acceptable form of birth control, and school nurses make regular visits to offer confidential advice.

We have, at the same time, seen an explosion of sexually explicit material in the media, which combines with this new ideology to stimulate a sexual awareness in children at an age when they are not yet emotionally mature enough to make appropriate choices. Stimulating our sexual desire is also a powerful means of keeping us distracted from rational reflection on what is happening around us, something we shall examine in more detail later. The reassurance from teachers that children should enjoy these sexual feelings may be at odds with the moral framework taught at home, and once more we see the distancing of parents from their children. The Christian understanding of freedom and self-responsibility to God has no place in an environment where children are encouraged to view sex as a form of self-gratification, a private choice without any reference to God or society outside of themselves. The notions of the "privacy of the bedroom" and "so long as it doesn't hurt anyone it must be okay" are the basis for the new morality, but in fact even from this perspective our children are being lied to.

There is a huge emphasis on "healthy living" in state schools today, much of it focussing on sports and diet. U.K. schools are required to demonstrate that they are including these topics in their curriculum, and the topics have been extended to include mental and emotional wellbeing. The great lie behind this is that homosexuality is taught to be an equal "lifestyle choice" to heterosexuality, and that children exhibiting homosexual tendencies are to be encouraged and supported in the natural choices they make. However, missing from the programmes' warnings about drugs, alcohol, tobacco and all the other dangerous activities children may be tempted to explore are the basic facts about homosexuality. "The Journal of the American Medical Association" revealed that homosexuality may shorten a person's life by as much as twenty percent. This research has been confirmed many times, including in the "International Journal of Epidemiology" (Oxford Academy) which stated in December 2001 that "nearly half of gay and bisexual men aged twenty will not reach their sixty-fifth birthday." The mortality rate due to treatment of HIV since 1996 has improved, but again in 2005 we read in "Psychological Reports" that life expectancy for homosexual men is twenty years shorter than for heterosexuals. The main cause of early death is sexually transmitted diseases, but homosexual lifestyles also result in them being twenty-four times more likely to commit suicide, and over a hundred times more likely to be murdered. "The Journal of the American Medical Association" found that fifty percent of males who are HIV positive admitted having had sex with an adult before the age of sixteen, and fifteen percent who were HIV positive revealed that they had had sex with an adult male by the time they were ten. These facts are never revealed to students because it is now unacceptable to suggest that the homosexual lifestyle is in any way negative, and yet schools promote lies when they ignore the dangers of premature death. Debates about homosexuality in the classroom are never focussed on disease and death, but on tolerance and human rights, framing the child's perspective very carefully so that acceptable conclusions are reached. To even suggest the real facts in a classroom would be enough for a teacher to lose their job: some truths must never be spoken.

The underlying issue here is the conflict between traditional Christianity and hedonism. Children are encouraged to see the concerns of their parents as the product of bigotry or a lack of awareness or from simply being old fashioned. Concerns about homosexuality, both from a moral and a health perspective are treated as homophobic, and the child is encouraged to doubt the wisdom of their parents, which can undermine everything being taught at home. State education is removing the ability of parents to bring up their children with their values, which is why the UN describes children as "social architects": of course, the children are nothing more than the building blocks in the hands of the real architects in the UN. A disturbing aspect of all this is that students are inevitably faced with questions about those groups which disagree with the schools' perspective, such as Christians, and of course, what should be done about them.

This supposedly "values neutral" education indoctrinates children into moral relativism, something which is the intended goal of a number of groups putting pressure on politicians to remove Christianity from our schools. It is not just the global agenda that threatens Christianity but national organisations too. On the National Secular Society's website we read "Our state schools are being transformed and exploited by evangelical groups as part of their missionary work." However, the Department of Education's response to this was "We have not seen any evidence to support these claims." The National Secular Society pretends to be promoting secularism, but in reality is pushing atheism. The claim that they are seeking to free education from religious belief is untrue: they wish to promote their own. This active group who often appear alongside politicians and religious leaders in television debates, can, as Ed West stated in an article published in the Telegraph, actually claim no greater membership than about seven thousand people: roughly the same as the British Sausages Appreciation Society.

One target of the Secular Society has been the Scripture Union, branded as an evangelical group intent on converting our youth. During my years as a teacher I saw them come to school once each year, politely lead an assembly, and offer a copy of the New Testament to anyone who wanted to take one. Their approach was quaint and conservative, they were harming no one, and students who did not share their beliefs were not forced to take a copy.

The Secular Society is not only concerned with restricting Christian groups' access to schools, but is intent on removing Christian schools from Britain altogether. On their website they state: "We think it is unjustifiable that a number of publicly funded schools with a religious designation (faith schools) are still permitted by law to teach RE from their own exclusive viewpoint. Such a situation not only undermines the integrity of the state education system, it also undermines young people's religious freedom."

We see here use of the word "still" to imply that their ideology is part of a modern movement away from these outdated approaches, and the focus is once more made to be about human rights as though their own atheist ideology is the truly liberating option to offer students. The site goes on to complain that RE teaching in schools "promotes religious belief": the intention is clear, to deny parents the right to educate their children according to their own religious convictions. This basic freedom is a human right the Secular Society does not consider protecting, they would rather the state had control over our children's faith. The British Humanist Association proudly announces on its website that it has had "numerous" meetings with the Department of Education to discuss the homophobia and creationist beliefs taught in some Christian schools", despite the fact that parents' right to raise their child with their own values is enshrined in law, even when those values do not conform to those of the wider society. Atheist pressure groups have access to our government and are being listened to; Christians should not be surprised when OFSTED begins to take a very critical view of faith schools. The methodology will be to criticise Islamic schools first, and use what they find there to attack the very notion of "religious" schools.

To say the teaching of religious education in U.K. schools is in crisis is something of an understatement. Almost all schools ignore the legal requirement to hold an assembly of a Christian nature each day, and OFSTED never criticises them for it during school inspections. But even many Christian teachers have found themselves conforming to a form of RE teaching that is little more than a kind of anthropology, a brief whistle-stop tour of various beliefs and practices in order to demonstrate how inclusive the school is. RE has become a form of sociology where no attempt is made to encourage students to explore their potential relationship with God.

Higher Education has been turned into a means of forcing people into debt. While the U.S. regularly tops the table for nations' spending on education (but constantly appears in the bottom half of the top forty developed countries in terms of academic achievement) the nation's students now owe over a trillion dollars in student-debt. It is no surprise that over seventy percent of college students who have graduated in the past three years do not have sufficient wealth to rent, let alone purchase their own accommodation.

In a single generation we have lost the sense of home and the community as an educational environment where it was unheard of for children to be developing completely independently of those closest to them. The home and community was where children traditionally learned social rules and morality (the prevalence of divorce and the break-down of the family unit is celebrated by many liberals as they see it creating a more tolerant and inclusive environment for children from broken homes). It is no accident that the gap between parents and children is growing, and that many of our teenagers exhibit forms of attention deficit and hyper activity that was unheard of thirty years ago. Children are becoming disassociated from anything having intrinsic value; the education received in our state schools does not lead them to any depth of thought or reflection. President Obama doubled the funding for the Centre for American Progress which on its own website states that "All children aged three and four should be able to voluntarily attend a full-day public pre-school programme", a programme heavily funded by the Soros Foundation. This is an attempt to separate parent and child during those formative years, when children are particularly vulnerable to manipulation. This is now combined with the effect of a dumbed-down media that promotes a carefully controlled outlook that if challenged will ridicule or demonise the challenger. Private management companies are acquiring ownership of our schools and the source of their money does not come under public scrutiny. Our democracy is dependent on a public that is able to question those in authority, and has the motivation to do so. Instead our children are being trained to be workers and consumers; the value of education is almost entirely linked with its capacity to ensure employment. Unless students are taught to value moral courage, to reject blind obedience and hold fast to their principles, then the global elite has an easier task in their enslavement. As Edward Everett famously said, "Education is a better safeguard of liberty than a standing army."

There is always going to be an inherent conflict between the humanistic view of man and

Christianity, and we see this conflict at work in our education system. As Christians we understand the purpose of education as being to enable us to fulfil God's will, and there is no legal requirement to send our children to a state school so long as we can demonstrate that they are receiving an education. The right to educate children must never be taken from parents, and the state must never be permitted to dictate the values and standards it believes supersede all other belief systems. Of course, Christian education must recognise the value of science and the humanities since all truth belongs to God and human expression in the arts is an important exploration of what it means to be created in God's image. The United Nations has been working for many decades to use our education systems to remove a sense of national identity, so that students will grow up willing to accept the justifications given for a single world government. Control of education predetermines many social and political concepts; it guides academic opinion and shapes public attitudes, it tells people what to think and for how long they should think it. But education in school is only one part of the programme, the attitudes and beliefs of the rest of us are manipulated in other ways. The issue is not what we think, but what we think we think: and where these thoughts originate.

Chapter 12 ~ Mind Control

Most of us assume that our ideas and attitudes are our own, that is, that we have formed them as a result of our experiences, beliefs, teachings and so on. We may be aware of certain schools of psychology that promote forms of behavioural determinism, whereby we are far more the product of our environment than the illusion of free will would have us believe, but on the whole, most of us would argue that we do have some degree of free will. Certainly, as Christians, we believe that we have moral responsibility for our actions and that we will be judged by God for our lives, and so few of us would be comfortable with the idea that our judgements are deliberately prompted and guided by others. And yet, for a number of decades, a great deal of research has been conducted to determine how far mass media influences people, and how to manipulate this influence. Even this, however, would not be too surprising to anyone who is aware of how the advertising industry uses psychological methods to encourage us to purchase particular products. But none of this comes close to the real extent of how far governments and other agencies attempt to control social norms and attitudes, and as we shall see, the reality is deeply disturbing. In this chapter we will look at some examples of mind control techniques that have been made public over recent years, but also at how the media is used as a powerful tool in maintaining control over the general population. We will examine the different types of thought manipulation that are used, and focus particularly on the most dangerous weapon of mind control in our enemy's arsenal: television.

Research into mind control is founded on ideas developed by Carl Yung, who himself was influenced by the occult teachings of his grandfather, the Freemason Carl Gustav. Yung's concept of archetypes presented those interested in manipulating the thought processes of the masses with a way of prompting specific reactions when people were exposed to particular symbols. This is the basis of occult imagery which is intended to trigger certain responses in the observer, but Yung's idea of the collective subconscious suggested the possibility that the technique could be used on whole populations. Throughout human history there have been attempts to control people's thought processes in this way. The Egyptian book of the Dead includes a number of rituals which are clearly intended to invoke trauma through torture and intimidation, and there are descriptions of potions used to alter subjects' states of mind.

Sigmund Freud's nephew, Edward Bernays, agreed with the idea that the general population is an irrational body that requires herding, he became known as the "father of public relations", and wrote

"The conscious and intelligent manipulation of the organised habits and opinions of the masses is an important element in democratic society. Those who manipulate this unseen mechanism of society constitute an invisible government which is the true ruling power of our country. We are governed, our minds are moulded, our tastes are formed, our ideas suggested, largely by men we have never heard of." (From "Propaganda"). It was Bernays who developed the concept of shopping for pleasure as a means of turning Americans into consumers, but his ideas were inevitably used by government agencies who had concerns that extended beyond selling cans of beans.

In 1939 meetings were held at the University of Chicago which were funded by the Rockefeller Foundation. The leading thinkers of the day in the fields of psychology and communications theories met in secret to discuss the impacts of various propaganda techniques. Amongst them was Harold Lasswell who argued that even in a so-called democratic society, the government would require an elite group who would control public attitudes through propaganda. In his Encyclopaedia of the Social Studies he warned that those ruling over us must not "succumb to democratic dogmatisms about men being the best judges of their own interests." As we shall see, during the following decades, this principle would be applied to the output of television and various other forms of media. But before we consider how this was achieved, let us look briefly at how the U.S. government has attempted to develop methods of controlling the human mind.

A number of projects run by the CIA are now out in the open. As early as 1952, with Project Moonstruck, attempts were being made to control subjects through electromagnetic implants in different parts of the head, in the hope of creating individuals capable of being used in covert operations. Perhaps the most famous of the CIA's projects, MK-Ultra, officially began a year after this. A number of books have been published on this subject, and of all the known mind control projects, this has become the most infamous because of the techniques it employed. It was an attempt to manipulate subjects through the use of drugs and electro-shock methods, and was aimed at programming behaviour without the subject being aware of what was done to them. A number of people have claimed to be victims of this procedure, and have described horrific acts of sexual abuse performed against them in order to induce Dissociative Identity Disorder; most famously by Cathy O'Brien who vividly describes her experiences in the book "Trance: Formation of America" (which was originally a presentation prepared for the U.S. House of Representatives Permanent Select Committee on Intelligence Oversight, but which was prevented from being heard for supposed reasons of national security). Commonly portrayed as multiple personality disorders, this condition permits the subject to function normally for many years, but when prompted, they are able to perform violent acts without later remembering having done them.

One of the early pioneers in this method was Joseph Mengele who conducted countless experiments on inmates at Auschwitz. At the end of the war, thousands of German scientists were taken to the U.S.A. as part of Operation Paperclip, though only those involved in the production of rockets, such as Warner Von Braun, were made public. The technique was also being advanced by the work of George Estabrooks, who in 1943 wrote in his book "Hypnotism" that the extent to which a person is susceptible to being hypnotised is directly related to their tendency to be vulnerable to dissociative states. It was later recognised that this disorder can often result from a traumatic experience, particularly childhood sexual abuse. The most extreme cases of the state result from extreme trauma, and Estabrook recognised that once an individual's core personality had been split in this way, it was relatively easy for someone to take control of one of the alter personalities. Estabrook noted that what is seen in those who have been exposed to severe trauma is exactly the same as that in someone who is hypnotised. Through systematic torture, the victim's ability to consciously process information is blocked. The traumatic state can cause the mind to create what are called "amnesia walls" which separate distinct parts of the mind from one another. In this way it is possible to create subjects whose walled-off personas can be triggered using certain stimuli such as music, key phrases, or sections of movies. The modern idea of retreating to a "happy place" in the mind when experiences are too painful mimics part of this process.

Many people who claim to have been abused as children while in the hands of the CIA have described the abuse taking place as part of satanic rituals, and it is a documented fact that the CIA played a part in the establishment of a number of satanic groups. We may interpret this in two ways, it may be that these groups formed a cover for the abuse of children, and increased the level of trauma experienced by the victim. Or it may be that there was a genuinely occult nature to their activities: we cannot prove which the case is. Freedom of information acts have revealed that the CIA kept children high on LSD for weeks at a time as part of their research, which will have made the subjects even more vulnerable. In order to undermine the accounts of the victims, the CIA has funded the False Memory Syndrome Foundation, which aims to dismiss most accounts of child abuse, not just those associated with the CIA. It is not surprising that some members of this foundation have been proven to be paedophiles, such as Paul and Shirley Ebele, authors of "The Politics of Child Abuse" who were discovered to be suppliers of child-pornography. In a later chapter we shall look in detail at how child abuse plays its part in the war against us.

Some of these details may be hard to accept, and perhaps we may not want to admit to ourselves that a government agency could conduct such vile experiments on children. But there is sufficient evidence to demonstrate without doubt that the children were subjected to sleep deprivation, electroshock therapy, an array of mind altering drugs, and intense physical pain which we would, in any other situation refer to as torture. The victims claim that they were also subjected to humiliation and physical mutilation as part of the process to break them down. Some claim that their CIA "handlers" would continue to monitor and abuse them for many years, even applying the treatment to the first generation of victims' children. The U.S. senate eventually forced the CIA to close the MK-Ultra project down in 1977; after twenty-four years of activity. However, a good amount of evidence has surfaced to show that the programme was simply switched and hidden, some believing it to now be called "Monarch", after the butterfly (for all of the symbolism of change and emergence that this brings).

These early projects were concerned with control of individuals, but demonstrate the interest the CIA had in mind control, and the steps they were willing to take to explore it. Other projects included the Trident Project, begun in 1989, the Tower Project, started in 1990, and HAARP, officially begun in 1995. What we observe is a move on from control of individuals to projects focussed on mass manipulation. For example, Project Clean Sweep is a project, started in 1997, which is concerned with manipulating the emotional response of the general population through the use of particular electromagnetic frequencies.

That these attempts to control us are being carried out should not come as any surprise. A hundred years ago those researching these techniques were far more open about their intentions and their philosophies. Walter Lippmann, the winner of two Pulitzer Prizes described the public as a "bewildered herd" which had to be controlled and guided by the ruling elite. He was expressing the beliefs of the elite themselves, who recognised mass media as a means of ruling without resort to violence. The concept at the heart of this philosophy became known as "manufacture of consent", which meant manipulating the public into agreeing with and accepting the agenda of the elite group. Lipmann wrote "The process by which public opinions arise, and the opportunities for manipulation, are open to anyone who understands the process." Lippmann was one of the founding members of the Council On Foreign Relations.

Clearly it is not possible to adopt the exact same approach to controlling the mind of a few individuals when attempting to do so to a whole population. The contemporary name for one aspect of the project is neuroscience. President Obama's government committed a hundred million dollars to the project under the title "BRAIN", which presented itself as an attempt to map the human brain for medical purposes. In other words, the hope was to be able to identify exactly where each of our emotional and psychological responses is based within the physiology of the brain. One aspect of BRAIN was to be able to eradicate memories so that people could be relieved of traumatic events in their past. While the claim was that it would grant relief to those suffering post-traumatic stress disorder, the real potential use of such an ability needs little imagination to conjure up. The goal of BRAIN is to provide a map of the brain that would enable others to be able to manipulate its functions through the activation or inhibiting of neurons. Perhaps we might judge any concern about this research as paranoid if it wasn't for the fact that so much of the funding comes directly from DARPA, which is the military research department of the U.S. government. A full knowledge of someone's brain activity has the potential to enable behavioural prediction, which undermines the notion of independent free will. Presenting the population with evidence that their free will is an illusion easily leads to the philosophy of complete slavery.

Let us briefly examine some of the key forms of thought manipulation being used on us. The first, and most widespread, we have already considered in some detail: education. One of the aims of all dictatorships is to assume control of the education system, and as we have identified, global foundations are spending vast sums to ensure that western education limits the awareness and capacity of children to reason, while preparing them for a life of work.

Alongside education we find the philosophy of consumerism, and it is no accident that many U.K. state schools are now inviting business leaders in to take assemblies and create the appropriate purpose and direction that young people perceive their education heading. Bernays recognised the need to undermine people's self-image in order to make them feel a need for certain products. But Bernays acknowledged that the techniques of advertising were also being used as propaganda by the government.

Governments recognised the need to give the masses something to cheer and cry about without them ever turning their collective energy against those in power. Sport has always been used as a means of keeping us distracted, and also directing the human tribal instincts into something controllable and harmless. Few people question why news broadcasts almost always conclude with sporting results, but not meaningful statistics such as regional road deaths or pay inequalities. Sporting triumphs are presented as national events, and while national sovereignty is being removed, the people are encouraged to shout for a particular coloured kit.

There is a growing body of evidence to support the idea that attacks are being made on our physical wellbeing. There are a number of pieces of research that have demonstrated that the fluoride added to our water inhibits thinking (and even lowers IQ levels). The growing psychiatry industry is particularly evident in the U.S.A. where we can see people being labelled with various disorders that were not known to exist twenty years ago. As a result, many Americans are prescribed medication to deal with what once would have been considered normal human anxieties. Perhaps most alarming of all is the fact that twenty-five percent of American children are now prescribed drugs for conditions which our grandparents would have suggested needed only fresh air and exercise to combat. The chemicals present in many fast and processed foods are another source of poison, and the combined effect is deterioration in both physical and mental states. One further aspect to this biological approach is the use of direct implants such as RFID chips, which are proclaimed as the solution to all kinds of problems such as lost children and locating workers in hostile environments. Some U.S. firms have already demanded that workers in their Mexican plants be chipped in order to monitor attendance, but their potential goes beyond these uses. As with many other innovations, it is in the military that we see the first widespread use, such as Verimed's chips used by the Israeli army. Scientists are discussing their potential use in rewiring the brain, and with the advancement of nanotechnology it is easy to foresee these pieces of equipment smuggled into our bodies through the food we eat, though we can only hope that this step is still some time away

There are studies claiming that we are being adversely affected by the electromagnetic waves that now fill the air around us. In all state schools Wi-Fi connection is required in every classroom, and it is feared by some researchers that this may alter the electromagnetic fields in the brain. The U.S. army has been conducting studies to examine how transcranial pulse ultra sound can be used to prevent unwanted emotional states in battle. Similarly, lethargy or fear may be produced in enemy soldiers, suggesting that the waves now pouring into our heads may not be as safe as we are told.

But the principle tool in guiding the opinions and thoughts of the masses is television. There are two main aspects to this, first what watching television does to the function of the brain, and then the content which is broadcast.

In 1969 Herbert Krugman, a psychologist completing research for General Electric (the company which owns NBC), found that within thirty seconds of a person watching television the functioning of the brain is completely altered. In a normal state the brain emits beta waves, but after just half a minute, the television watching brain switches to the emission of alpha waves. Only when the subjects in his experiments moved away from the television and began reading did the brain resume its normal function. This is an extremely important discovery, one which has been reproduced many times by other researchers. It is important because the emission of beta waves is associated with reasoning and logical thought. The brain emits alpha waves when it is in a day-dream like state, or when someone has been hypnotised. Someone watching television is therefore known to be in a far more receptive state, since they will absorb suggestions from the television directly into their subconscious mind. By presenting archetypal imagery, or simply positive ones such as a mother with her baby, it is known that the brain emitting alpha waves is far more likely to respond in predicted patterns.

Studies have found that by monitoring the electrical patterns in the brain when watching television, the higher levels of functioning, such as in the neocortex, close down. This means information is being received by the brain but not analysed: it is like opening the front door of our minds to allow anyone in. Alpha waves are also associated with pronounced memory retention, which means that which is implanted may be effective over many years.

It is known that people who suffer with ADHD are already producing too much alpha, and so watching television will further accentuate their problem. But it has also been shown that when watching television our bodies can produce adrenaline when stimulated by appropriate imagery, and also stress hormones. The quick changing visuals are not naturally experienced, and they trigger the brain's "orienting response", which is a survival instinct over which we have no conscious control, but which keeps our attention focussed on what is before us in case of threat. We can thus become transfixed by television, staring at the screen without making a choice to do so. This is why we may find our focus in a post office queue drawn to a screen regardless of whether we wish to look at it. A further biological response to television can be the release of endorphins, to which the body can become addicted. The removal of a child's television may cause a tantrum which is the addict's cry for his fix. In the U.S. it is estimated that the majority of children spend between four and five hours each day in front of a screen, whether that be television or a computer game, and despite what gamers may say, the effect is as bad from both. It is known that this amount of time in front of a screen is a cause of obesity, disruption of sleep patterns and a willingness to participate in risky behaviour (such as inappropriate sexual activity). Television causes the brain to shift from left to right side dominance, which is the shift from rational to emotional and non-critical function. Krugmann observed that the television watcher responds to the medium, not to the content, and is thus vulnerable to considerable manipulation.

The illusion of a picture on our television screen is exactly that, an illusion. The mind perceives a picture that does not really exist at any one time, since what the brain perceives is really a series of dots flashing on and off thirty times per second. This is known as the "flicker-effect", and studies have shown that though we cannot consciously register the flicker, the body is responding to it. As J. Mander points out in his book "Four Arguments For The Elimination of Television", we normally perceive images outside in reality, but when watching television, the image only truly exists in the mind. We are not able to perceive what is happening to us since the brain and eye are not capable of processing information at this unnatural speed: and so the television watcher is allowing the screen to project non-existent images into the mind itself. The level of trust the watcher exhibits in this process is astonishing – or would be if they knew what was happening.

As we have noted, it is not only the physiological impact of television we should be concerned about, but also what is being broadcast. Children today are exposed to tens of thousands of advertisements on television every year: that is more than a person living sixty years ago saw in their whole lifetime. Companies select when their advertisements will be broadcast according to viewing figures, and so media companies are always seeking the greatest share of the viewing public. This results in output that is by nature unchallenging or intellectually undemanding, and anything that may be socially contentious is avoided. At the same time, the more frivolous or sexually stimulating the content is, the greater the viewing figures (pornography is the number one item searched for on the internet).

Television could be a source of alternative viewpoints and opinions about life and morality, but it isn't. A pretence is made of presenting disagreements and debates, but in reality all viewpoints expressed fall within narrow margins of acceptable ideas. This is because the number of companies who own the media has shrunk to very few. In the U.S. over the last twenty years the number of media outlets has fallen from fifty to just five. A wide selection of names is given to various

226

production companies, giving the impression that a variety of voices are being heard, but they are all owned by the same small elite groups. For example, AOL Time Warner owns: CNN; HBO; the Cartoon Network; Warner Bros; Cinemax; TNT, as well as sixty-four different magazines such as Time, Life, MAD and DC Comics, along with over forty music labels including Elektra and Atlantic. It was inevitable that this consolidation of media corporations would result in a uniform world view coming from them. The variety of media owned by these few companies also guarantees that the same message is heard coming from the television, the radio, the newspapers, music and so on. This results in a standardisation of thought, a single world view that becomes the norm amongst the masses since it is heard coming from every source. It becomes difficult for most people to question, let alone reject the self-evident norms presented on the news, in soap operas and on Radio Four. Alternative voices are ridiculed and easily made to look bizarre or extreme since all the well-spoken personalities we have come to know and trust are telling us to think this way. An example of this has been the introduction of trans-gender identity to British culture. In 2015 I began to notice news items appearing on BBC radio about trans-gender people. At the time I hardly knew what the term meant. Within two years television programmes and political debates were full of references to trans-gender rights, and it was easy to see how the media had slowly introduced the issue before developing it as a mainstream idea. This suggestive programming is also at play with regards to the elimination of cash. As mentioned earlier, from 3rd to 7th April 2017, BBC Radio Four ran nightly items on its evening news questioning whether we need to continue with physical money. The items including journalists asking people if they "still" used cash, and each night one of the presenters would refer to cash as "old fashioned". The items were clearly intended to sow the first seeds which will later be raised without too much negative reaction since we have been made to see that this is an issue to be debated. Had the question simply been dropped on people, a more forceful rejection might have occurred. This predictive programming is used to guide acceptance of where the elite wishes society to go, core messages are made so uniform and presented in gradual steps so that while an illusion of choice is maintained, the outcomes are always inevitable. In this way, even an agenda which goes against the interests of the masses will be accepted through continual and gradual introduction. Another aspect is the systematic desensitisation of the public to an agenda that might otherwise have provoked shock or revulsion. For example, every form of light entertainment, including soap operas and panel shows, will have at least one gay character, portrayed from a positive perspective. Once the public has grown to know and like the characters, it is easier to introduce legislation such as same sex "marriage" for which the public has steadily been prepared in order for it to appear morally correct.

Television promotes a materialistic world view; it aims to convince us that we are living in a Godless reality and that we are free to pursue our own self-centred desires. Morally corrupting figures are presented as role models, and the greater the level of degeneracy the more they are applauded and celebrated. Situation comedies present characters who happily revel in their hatred of books and ordinary people are encouraged to identify with crude and ignorant characters so that they become numbed and unreflective. Another pattern we see repeated many times is the portrayal of Christians as joyless busy-bodies. In the U.K. series EastEnders, the character Dot Cotton was a bitter old woman who regularly referred to Bible texts in her complaints. We see the same type of character in the Australian soap Neighbours, creating the attitude amongst viewers that Christianity is for hypocrites. Today the soaps have moved on in their portrayal, and in a number of series we find Anglican ministers who are gay. While there are homosexuals amongst the Church of England clergy, the media presentation of them is wholly disproportionate. It is not only through the popular entertainment programmes that we are being misled. In the 1960s and '70s Walter Cronkite delivered the news on the most popular news broadcasts in America on CBS TV. He became a trusted source of information for millions of people who believed that he was presenting the facts as they were, independently of political bias. However, in his introduction to the book "Censored – The News That Didn't Make The News – And Why" he wrote "A handful of us determine what will be on the evening news broadcasts, or for that matter the New York Times, The Washington Post or Wall Street Journal; it is a handful of us with this awesome power. We must decide from hundreds of stories which we will expose that day. And those available to us have already been culled and re-culled by persons far outside our control." Today the news programmes present the exact same stories from the same viewpoint: the agreed omission of stories is the real trick. In 2017 the BBC had a series of programmes focussing on "Fake News" because the internet has opened up an array of alternative viewpoints that often directly contradict the narrative presented by the mainstream media. There is a clear attempt to discredit these alternative voices, and pressure is being applied to have stories removed from social media sites if they do not conform to the version of events found in the propaganda. This pressure has already had results in Germany where Facebook has been fined for allowing users to publish unwanted information. Cronkite gave a speech to the World Federalists Association when he was receiving an award; in it he said "It seems to many of us that if we are to avoid the eventual catastrophic world conflict we must strengthen the United Nations as a first step toward a world government. Our failure to live up to our obligation to the UN is led by a handful of wilful senators who choose to pursue a narrow objective. They pander to and are supported by the Christian Coalition and the rest of the religious right wing." Cronkite knew only too well that the removal of the Church in America will be a necessary step to fulfil the elite's agenda, but these views were never revealed on his nightly broadcasts.

Though television is an invasive presence in most homes, the enormous budgets available to Hollywood film makers provides another powerful set of tools to exert pressure on the minds of the masses. Movies have always been a means of determining social attitudes, while producers and directors have presented their work as self-expression and art. Harold Lasswell described how the real meaning or message of a movie can only be understood consciously when we identify the use of symbols in the imagery. He said that by identifying the frequency and intensity of the use of particular symbolism the real purpose of the movie can be understood. While movie-goers think they are enjoying the surface story and characters, the real message is inserted into the unconscious mind in order to direct attitudes towards a chosen subject. For example, once the moral standing of a character is established, their actions or speech can subtly prompt a negative or positive reaction according to the film-makers intention. Edward Bernays declared that "The American motion picture is the greatest unconscious carrier of propaganda in the world today. It is a great distributor for ideas and opinions. The motion picture can standardise the ideas and habits of a nation."

Hollywood was established by Ashkenazi Jewish immigrants who quickly established control through what became known as the studio system. One of the consequences of this demographic is that while Christian symbols are frequently debased in movies, we never see the bad guy wearing a Star of David around his neck. There are also many portrayals of savage and unhinged Christian priests, but rabbis escape with nothing more than the occasional joke aimed at them (but nothing too cutting). All Jewish imagery is treated with great respect by Hollywood, since it is a Jewish understanding of political correctness that always prevails. This includes promoting abortion, homosexuality and the removal of prayers from schools (changes which the general population are left imagining simply appeared out of thin air). Over sixty percent of Hollywood movies are produced or owned by Jews (who make up less than three percent of the general population). This imbalance has enabled Zionists to use the medium to endorse their politics and attack all opposition; it gives them a powerful tool in influencing public attitudes. Examples of this include the constant representation of Arabs as untrustworthy or terrorists, and the association of being pro-Palestinian as anti-Semitic. There is barely a week of television that does not pass without some reminder of the Holocaust, reinforcing the sense of Jews as victims, while few average T.V. watchers will be made aware of the twenty million Russians killed by their Communist government. In fact, since the end of the Second World War, more than two hundred and eighty million people have been killed in wars, but Hollywood and television primarily focus on the numbers killed in Nazi Germany. Even to question this bias is at risk of being labelled anti-Semitic and so few public voices dare mention it.

In 2015 WikiLeaks published a number of emails as a result of a hack into Sony's computers. Amongst the finds were a series of emails revealing the plan to promote a positive image of Israel to counter balance the growing world-wide concern over the slaughter of Palestinians that Summer. Further analysis of the documents revealed a pattern of support for Israel's policies and a widespread support for Zionism amongst

Hollywood's elite and powerful. Implicated in the emails were actresses Natalie Portman and Scarlett Johansson, as well as a number of producers who discussed creating an anti-Palestinian documentary which would undermine its hopes of statehood. The leaks revealed a deliberate promotion of stories which highlighted anti-Semitic attacks, and the intention of linking them with opposition to Israel. In one email, Hollywood producer Ron Rotholz states his belief that "recognition of Hamas as a legitimate government with legitimate policies and a legitimate charter, by western governments is a hate crime on a global scale."

That the movie industry is being used as propaganda is clear, but let us pause for a moment to consider what kind of message is being delivered. In the 1940s and 50s divorce was unheard of amongst most ordinary people in the U.K., but it was nothing unusual to read of movie stars entering a second or third marriage. Actors were used as role models in all kinds of ways, not least to undermine the idea of marriage being a life-long commitment. At first this might strike us as a curious goal, but as we shall see in a later chapter, one of the objectives of the elite is the destruction of the family.

The culture of Hollywood is one of hedonism and self-promotion. Drug use by celebrities and film producers has been documented as widespread by numerous sources. Along with the drugs, prostitution and paedophilia is also rampant. Actor Woody Harrelson stated in USA Weekend in 1996, "Every acting business I ever entered into in New York seemed to have a casting couch. I've seen so many people sleep with people they loathe in order to further their ambition." But this abuse of power extends to children in Hollywood. Actor Corey Feldman was interviewed about his experiences as a child star by Fox News, he said "I can tell you that the number one problem in Hollywood was and is and always will be paedophilia." Another actor, Elijah Wood, confirmed this in a 2016 interview with the Sunday Times when he stated "a lot of vipers are preying on children in the business." Once we recognise the true moral character of Hollywood, we must question the kinds of moral truths that are being communicated in movies, and what kinds of role models the film industry is setting before young people (who are the principle target of Hollywood films today).

The link between Hollywood and occultism has been well documented. For example, the founder of the "Church of Satan", Anton Szandor LaVey, who promoted the ideas of U.K. occultist Aleister Crowley, is known to have had strong ties with a number of producers, writers, directors and actors in the mid to late sixties. Accounts of orgies were well known at the time, and some of the celebrities involved with him were often quite open about some of their activities, such as Sammy Davis Jr.

(who took to painting one of his fingernails black as a sign of membership) and Jayne Mansfield. One of the results of this connection was the film "Rosemary's Baby" released in 1968, in which director Roman Polanski had LaVey play the devil when he rapes the character played by Mia Farrow (one-time wife of Davis' fellow "Rat Packer" Frank Sinatra). Some might dismiss it as coincidence, but Farrow was to head out to India that same year to learn transcendental meditation with The Beatles, who themselves had chosen to have Aleister Crowley's picture appear on the cover of their album "Sergeant Pepper's Lonely Hearts Club band" which was released in 1967. By 1969, however, the interest people in Hollywood were willing to show publicly was reduced when Roman Polanski's pregnant wife, Sharon Tate, was ritualistically murdered by members of Charles Manson's gang, the "Family". One of the murderers was a woman called Susan Atkins who had been a topless dancer for one of LaVey's events. Polanski has spent the last four decades on the run in Europe to evade arrest for charges of paedophilia. LaVey died in 1997, but his satanic organisation continues. Today, however, in keeping with the mood of the times, the "Church of Satan" describes itself as a group for "sceptical atheists", and is involved in promoting women's rights and the right to abortion on demand.

While Hollywood is more careful today in the way it portrays itself, it continues to promote occultism. In an episode of the children's programme "The Simpsons" the character portrayed as the free-thinking intellectual of the family, Lisa, encountered and showed great sympathy towards a group that revealed itself to be Wiccans. The group of girls were portrayed sympathetically, as opposed to the hypocritical Christian minister in the series, and for many children this will have been their first exposure to Wicca. In reality, the man responsible for its revival in America, Gerald Gardner, admits to a fascination with the teachings and rituals of Aleister Crowley, who he knew and who had made him an honorary member of his magic order. Gardner incorporated many of Crowley's rituals into the version of Wicca that has become so widespread in the U.S. today. Crowley's system of what he called "magik" involved inviting demons to make themselves present and offering sacrifices in exchange for their assistance.

While many see the objection to the Harry Potter series of films as the product of Evangelical extremism, the number of internet searches for "witchcraft" and "Wicca" rises around and after the release of each new book and film. The intention is to present witches/occultists as exciting, decent, and a source of escapism. Unlike the books of Tolkein and C. S. Lewis which create an entirely fictional world, Rowling instead inserts the actual rituals and practices of occultists into her books, so that children read of a parallel world rather than one that is based in fantasy. Rowling admits to her careful research into the occult, and we find countless examples of real occult techniques presented in her book as fiction. For example, in Harry Potter, Prisoner Of Azkaban we find a very accurate description of occult techniques, she writes: "fortune telling is an extremely refined art. We'll start by the relaxation of the mind and of the eyes in order to clear our interior eye and the superconscience." (page 297). Rowling even introduces a character called Cassandra Vlabatsky, who is clearly based on H.P. Blavatsky, discussed earlier in this book.

Crowley's often repeated motto was "do what thou wilt shall be the sum of the law". In other words, he presented freedom as following whatever impulses or desires we might have, and that to suppress them is to be enslaved: the exact opposite of Christ's teaching. The phrase became LaVey's motto too, and is still declared by Crowley's cult called "Ordo Templi Orientis" (OTO) which continues today. Jimmy page, of the rock group Led Zeppelin, owned a bookshop in London selling many OTO books, and his interest led him to purchase Crowley's home, Boleskine House, on the banks of Loch Ness. The daughter of Bob Geldof, the singer behind the charity event Live Aid, had an "OTO" tattoo, and on her Twitter account encouraged her young fans to read Crowley's books (sadly, she is now dead).

We should not be surprised that occultists should seek to spread their worldview through films, they have always used whatever medium is available, be that paintings, drama, sculpture or music. In the early days of Hollywood, films presented the idea of the lone hero, separate from society, who achieves his goals through force of will. With time this has evolved so that in many films today, the hero is portrayed saving humanity through his development of special, often supernatural powers. What would have been wholly unacceptable to audiences fifty years ago has now become mainstream. The hero in many fantasy and sci-fi movies ushers in a new age of freedom; it is clearly programming the popular mind to accept the idea of the one who is to come to change the world. Even children's films are full of pagan magic and various occult practices and symbols, carefully guiding our next generation into a satanic way of thinking. The barriers to accepting a false messiah are being broken down, and when he comes he will be received and understood from the context of years of subliminal preparation.

So we see that interest in occultism amongst film makers and musicians is nothing new, neither has it gone away. But so long as the general population can be kept docile and passive, then we will be receptive to the coordinated script that has been used for a long time. We are being conditioned to not only accept a single world government, but to consider it desirable and preferable. We have entered a new stage where the elite are no longer relying on systems of propaganda, but have begun to explore direct physical alteration of the brain. Companies like Google and Microsoft are investing unimaginable sums into ways of merging reality with virtual reality, what they refer to as "augmented reality" which will enable a rewiring of the brain to facilitate greater thought control. Many people are being forced to work longer hours at the end of which they collapse, exhausted in front of their televisions. Research which began as ways to manipulate these tired people into buying products has been adopted by those who intend to enslave us. As we are desensitised to what is to come, the agenda is slowly revealed, Bailey's "externalisation of the hierarchy". It is done within a total environment which makes the propaganda invisible, while it triggers our basic needs and instincts to prompt the right irrational response. No longer is there any need for subliminal messages, the content is right before our eyes, but we have been sucked so deeply beneath the dark surface of their pool we can no longer see what it is that drowns us. The systems of mind control are already dominating the choices we make about the food we eat, the perception we have of the world around us, our origins as human beings, but the real goal is to destroy our ability to choose obedience to Christ.

Chapter 13 ~ Child Abuse

For most of us, the term child abuse is associated with individuals within families or places of work. But the reality is that children have and are being sexually abused in huge numbers, while various institutions either sanction or ignore what is happening. We have already seen how U.S. agencies have used child abuse as part of their attempts to create methods of mind control. But now we shall consider three other institutions where the evidence points to a systematic cover-up of what is taking place.

Many British people have become aware of paedophiles who have been working for the BBC, such as Jimmy Savile and Rolf Harris, and how they were allowed to abuse their victims with apparent immunity from even criticism from their bosses. While the BBC claims it was unaware of what was happening within its organisation, many who had contact with it or worked directly for it have since stated that it was common knowledge that children were not safe around these men. These high-profile cases involving celebrities have forced U.K. news organisations to deal with the issue, and this has led to a stream of victims feeling confident enough to admit what was done to them. The subsequent public outcry has forced the British establishment into answering questions about the abuse of children within Westminster and by high-ranking politicians. It has been discovered that as early as 1982, Conservative Home Secretary Leon Brittan was presented with files containing details of paedophiles working within and around the government. However, when a later inquiry was ordered to investigate these claims, it was found that one hundred and fourteen files had gone missing. As Keith Vaz (who himself was later discovered to be using male escorts) said, it was the loss of files on an "industrial scale". This deliberate destruction of evidence has never been explained, although when asked about it on the Andrew Marr show, Norman Tebbit admitted that "at the time, most people would have thought the establishment, the system, was to be protected." Labour M.P. Simon Danczuk, who investigated the child abuse in care homes carried out by Liberal M.P. Cyril Smith, described the problems he faced when trying to find the truth, he said "The mood is dominated by silence." We should note that, like Jimmy Savile, Cyril Smith received a knighthood (in 1988), even though Margaret Thatcher was warned about allegations made against him (Lord Armstrong had also warned Thatcher of Savile's activities back in 1998, but again she went ahead with approving his knighthood).

The lawyer representing abuse victims, Alison Millar, acknowledged that there was "a growing suspicion amongst the electorate that there is a conspiracy over the abuse of children by those with great power." She even went as far as to say that "the allegations are so serious, and go so far up in the government, to make many survivors fear for their safety." That a paedophile ring in Westminster should be so powerful as to make victims fear they might be murdered if they identified the perpetrators of these acts reveals the extent to which the problem is enmeshed within the establishment. When labour M.P. John Mann had been working as a Lambeth Councillor, he says cases of abuse he presented to the police were not pursued because the police claimed their enquiries were prevented from continuing on the orders of their superiors.

A number of politicians have claimed that the rumours of abuse were not acted upon because it was simply a different age with a different culture back then: the kind of culture that would turn a blind eye to child sexual abuse we can only imagine. But there was certainly a different political stance amongst left wing politicians who viewed individual freedom as the ultimate human goal. As a result, future cabinet ministers Harriet Harman and Patricia Hewitt felt it acceptable to work for the National Council For Civil Liberties (which today has changed its name to "Liberty") which was affiliated with the Paedophile Information Exchange which openly argued for the legitimacy of adults having sex with children. This is an important detail; we must understand that there are powerful people who sanction groups such as these, it isn't simply a lone pervert within a family, it is an organised attempt to change social attitudes in order to make child abuse an acceptable activity.

On the international stage we also find the United Nations demonstrating at best, an utter disregard for the well-being of children. Between December 2013 and June 2014, French soldiers serving as part of a UN exercise in the Central African Republic were discovered to be raping young boys who had been picked up by patrols or who had approached the troops in search of food. When Anders Kompass, the director of field operations at the UN rights office in Geneva discovered what was happening, he tried to work within the UN to stop it. But his efforts were ignored and suppressed by the UN, forcing him to go public and provide French prosecutors with the evidence he had found. While the UN continued to publicly declare it had a "zero tolerance" over child abuse, it attempted to sanction Kompass for breaking UN policy by making the facts public. As a result, journalists discovered that cases of child abuse by UN peacekeepers existed in Kosovo, Bosnia, the Democratic Republic of Congo, and many other places. The UN's witch-hunt to silence whistle-blowers reveals the true attitude towards this issue, but we may interpret it in different ways. It may be that the UN persists with the same approach as the British establishment, in that the reputation of the organisation is considered more important than the lives of children. Or it may point to something more sinister, the existence of a more systematic and widespread abuse of children that involves major organisations.

Before looking at the most dramatic and evil example of this, let us pause to remember the example of the abduction, rape and murder of many children in Belgium which clearly pointed to a network of paedophiles that included powerful people. Marc Dutroux and his wife were first convicted of the rape and abduction of five children in 1989. Despite the abuse of their victims being extremely violent, Dutroux was sentenced to just thirteen years and was released after serving just three. Perhaps we might imagine that prison had transformed him to such a degree that the Belgian authorities were demonstrating an appropriate level of compassion. However, we discover that the prison governor with responsibility for him, Yvan Stuaert, revealed that a medical report written during his incarceration described Dutroux as "a perverse psychopath. An evident danger to society." Interestingly, the man who made the decision to have Dutroux released was the Justice Minister Melchior Wathelet, who went on to become a judge at the European Court of Justice at The Hague.

It was not long after Dutroux's release that young girls began to go missing once more. Police did not wonder how a man who was unemployed could own six homes, in the vicinity of which children were disappearing. Dutroux's own mother informed police that he had secret cells built beneath his homes, and that she knew a child was being held there. The police ignored this information as well as other informants' tips; they even heard a child beneath the floor during an inspection of one of his homes but failed to investigate the source. Dutroux was permitted to go on abducting girls to order for another four years before he was once more arrested. Subsequently, the L.A. Times revealed that the children's activist Marie-France Botte claimed that the Belgian Justice Ministry had in its possession a list of clients for whom Dutroux was providing tapes of his victims' suffering that included many high level businessmen and political figures. This was supported by information obtained during the interrogation of one of Dutroux's accomplices, a businessman called Jean-Michael Nihoul, who admitted helping to organise an orgy where children were abused which was attended by a former European Commissioner as well as high ranking police officers. During his trial, Dutroux threatened to "bring down the government and the entire state" by naming his clients. Subsequently, nine police officers and three magistrates were investigated as being part of the network. Dutroux stated in a later interview that an international paedophile network existed but that authorities demonstrated no interest in pursuing the information he provided.

The outrage expressed by Belgians over this case was understandable, but the media coverage has carefully determined a public perception of the case as being solved, and that a particular paedophile has been imprisoned. But while this case has been managed by those in power, the abuse of children by Roman Catholic priests has been happening in so many countries over such a long period of time, that even the power of the Vatican has not been able to suppress it. The L.A. Times revealed that since 1960, ten percent of all graduates from Saint John's Seminary, one of the largest Roman Catholic seminaries in the U.S., have been paedophiles. This means one in ten of the priests leaving this institution have been abusing children: in terms of sexual abuse, there can be no organisation on earth which is more of a threat to our children than the Roman Catholic Church. But this raises two principle questions: why are there so many paedophiles amongst Roman Catholic clergy, and why has the institution protected them and even bullied victims into silence?

The prevalence of paedophile Roman Catholic clergy is a complicated issue. In the documentary "Deliver Us From Evil" the lawyers and psychologists point to an unhealthy attitude which is developed amongst seminarians towards all forms of sex. Since compulsory chastity makes sexual relationship with a woman a sin, it becomes no more of a sin from this distorted perspective to engage in a sexual relationship with a child. Though most normal people would find this perspective abhorrent, many seminarians enter their training at such a young age that their sexual development is stunted, and this, the documentary proposes, contributes to so many of them being paedophiles.

While this may play its part, there is another aspect to the whole issue which even critical observers are often wary of mentioning because it sits so uncomfortably with the modern liberal attitude towards sexuality. The vast majority of victims of Roman Catholic paedophiles have been teenage boys, something which contradicts the technical definition of paedophilia which describes it as an "obsessive sexual attraction to children". In reality these Roman Catholic clergy are not generally attracted to all children, but specifically to young males.

Research shows that between one quarter and one half of all Roman Catholic clergy are homosexual. It is not a comfortable statement for many people to read, but the truth is that male sexuality is inherently promiscuous by nature: during a placement as part of my training at Anglican theological college in 1992 I worked at a centre for homosexual men who were HIV positive. I was struck by the immense number of sexual partners the men had had (and were still having despite their diagnosis). This permissive attitude to sexuality inevitably leads to promiscuity existing within seminaries where not only the students are gay, but many of the priests in charge. In "The Changing Face of the Priesthood", Father Donald Cozzens, who himself had been the head of a Roman Catholic seminary, described the Roman clergy as becoming "a gay profession". For those gay men who entered the seminary young with their own sexuality so undeveloped, and which finds expression within a homosexual culture in the seminary, it should not be surprising that once out in the ministry, teenage boys often become the focus of their sexual feelings.

We might wonder why so many homosexuals are drawn to the priesthood in the first place. For a profession that insists on compulsory chastity, a gay man is actually sacrificing much less than a heterosexual man, since the latter will have to forego marriage and a family, while a gay man would have had to hide his sexual activity within a Roman Catholic culture, whether he was a layman or part of the clergy. Homosexual culture is now so dominant amongst Roman Catholic clergy that Father Andrew Greeley famously dubbed it "the lavender mafia".

But even knowing this, we might ask why so many Roman Catholic clergy become paedophiles. Once more, the facts make uncomfortable reading for those who wish to hide behind a politically correct mind-set. The Journal of Sex Research found that one third of all sex offences against children are committed by gay men. While heterosexuals do commit more of the total number, since homosexuals make up less than four percent of the total population, this means that this tiny minority of men is committing one third of all the offences. This disproportionately high figure means a gay man is far more likely to be a paedophile than a man who is heterosexual.

A further aspect to this is that while some gay men abuse children in order to gratify their desires, Steve Baldwin noted in an article published by Regent University law Review that within the homosexual culture there is a deliberate intention to target children in order to enlarge the homosexual movement. The mainstream media remains silent on this because of its fear of the liberal establishment, but also because of the direct influence homosexuals have in the media. For example, The National Lesbian and Gay Journalists Association rejoiced at the fact that three quarters of those who choose what makes the front page of the New York Times are gay. This is why Roman Catholic abusers are never referred to as gay, and the homosexual nature and motive of their crime is never discussed.

Homosexual culture is extremely youth orientated, and many leading gay publications carry advertisements for holiday destinations such as Burma, Sri Lanka and the Philippines, where young male prostitutes are available. In the U.S. there exists an organisation called The North American Man-Boy Love Association which specifically promotes homosexual paedophilia. And while these groups openly acknowledge their intention, when child sexual abuse cases are dealt with by the police and the courts, it is very rare for a child molester to be identified as a homosexual.

In terms of world-wide child trafficking, boys represent half of all victims, despite the popular image presented being one of girls and women. Boys are known to constitute fifty percent of all victims of child sexual exploitation, which makes no sense when we know that homosexuals represent such a tiny portion of the population. At least, it makes no sense if we continue to deny the facts about homosexual abusers. To further add to their suffering, the U.S. Department of Justice found that the majority of underage boys arrested for involvement in prostitution are far more likely to be charged rather than being brought to the attention of care services, as happens with young girls. But NGOs have found that the donations they receive from the public and governments are much higher when they portray themselves working with vulnerable girls and women rather than boys.

Even if we were to accept that this huge number of paedophile Roman Catholic priests was abusing children because they had somehow been victimised by others or by their experiences in the seminaries, it still would not account for the response of the institution itself to the suffering of their victims. An evil act performed by one man may be understood in terms of weakness, or illness, but when the Roman Catholic Church repeatedly chooses to protect its own reputation and the careers of its clergy while intimidating victims in order to silence them, something beyond individual weakness emerges. Let us consider the case of Father Oliver O'Grady, an Irishman who worked in California. His diocese became aware that he was a paedophile in 1973, and despite many victims and their families making complaints about him for decades, he was simply moved from one parish to another, where he was free to continue his abuse and rape of children. Bishop Roger Mahoney assured victims that he was being moved to where he would have no further contact with children, but each time he went into another parish. Bishop Mahoney was rewarded for his protecting of the Roman Catholic Church's good name with a promotion to the status of Cardinal Bishop, while hundreds of children were abused by Father O'Grady.

The institutional involvement goes beyond the level of diocesan bishops. From 1978 to 2005, Cardinal Ratzinger had the role of overseeing what we would today call child protection. Despite the ongoing abuse and attempts to cover-up what was happening, the cardinal later became Pope Benedict XVI. His role in the suppression of information and his failure to protect children resulted in legal accusations of conspiracy to cover-up sexual abuse. In order to escape prosecution and avoid unwanted publicity, the Vatican applied for and was granted by President George W. Bush immunity from prosecution for the Pope. Why the U.S. government was willing to comply is unclear.

It is estimated that there are now over a hundred thousand victims of Roman Catholic Clergy abuse in the U.S. alone: and we can assume that the true figure is much higher since psychologists tell us that eighty percent of victims of sexual abuse never come forward. Many countries around the world are now beginning to discover the extent of this problem, and the historical cases point to a long-standing reality that has been concealed from the public until now. There can be no excuses made for any organisation that puts its own position of power and worldly reputation before the safety of children. But an organisation doing this and claiming to be the Church of Christ is committing evil. We cannot know the emotional and psychological damage caused by Roman Catholic clergy, and we cannot begin to guess at how many people have turned away from Christ because they believed the claim that this is the Church. Let us be clear, Rome is not the Church, nor is it a part of the Church. The fruit we see Rome bearing is not of the Holy Spirit, it is not the fruit of grace.

When social workers claimed that they had uncovered many children in Cleveland, in the U.K., who had been abused as part of satanic rituals, the media mocked them as hysterical; it seemed unbelievable that in the 1980s people could be doing this. But as we have learned, child abuse is often an aspect of worldly power that must be recognised as a genuine phenomenon. There exist networks of powerful people in different organisations that have been so corrupted that children are considered by them to have no value beyond the means to which they can be used as a source of self-gratification. Well-respected institutions, people honoured with titles and awards, are all proven to be part of this activity, protected by the law and concealed from the public by a disinterested media. This debasement and corruption of children is a powerful sign of the true nature of the elite powers that control the world.

Chapter 14 ~ The Council On Foreign Relations

So many of the different strands we have examined so far connect in The Council On Foreign Relations (CFR). This is the organisation that acts as the intermediary between so many elite groups: the bankers, international corporations, oil companies and governments. The CFR's members take their place in which ever U.S. administration happens to be in power, whether Republican or Democrat, returning to their corporate jobs once their term is over. The facts about the CFR reveal how they have influenced U.S. policy, both domestic and foreign, and how the illusion of democracy is maintained to shield the people in power from public scrutiny.

Although the official story of the CFR begins just after World War I, when business and banking leaders recognised the growing threat of socialism in the U.S., the real origins are to be found much earlier. Following the Napoleonic Wars, the Rothschilds were behind the establishment of the Congress of Vienna which was an attempt to deal with the debts and international conflict. European heads of state were offered an opportunity to deal with their debts by submitting to what was in effect, an early form of the League of Nations. However, the Russian Tsar recognised what was happening and prevented the plot from being carried through: an act of defiance that would not be avenged until 1917. In 1910 the minutes of the trustees for the Carnegie Endowment for International Peace include the statement "Is there any way known to man more effective than war, to so alter the life of an entire people?" In order to achieve the ability to involve the U.S. in whichever wars it intended, the trustees recognised that they must take control of U.S. diplomats and the State Department. World War I had produced an enormous national debt: which translated as huge profits for the banks. It wasn't until 1918 that an elite group of one hundred and eight bankers, lawyers and businessmen grouped together with the Andrew Carnegie lawyer Elihu Root as their head, initially known as the Institute for International Affairs. The formation of this new organisation was driven by Edward House, who had been instrumental in creating the Federal Reserve, U.S. income tax and had even been the man to come up with the name "League of Nations". It was House who proposed the plan to infiltrate both the Republican and Democrat parties, while giving the public a sense of choosing one or the other. Since 1940 for example, every Secretary of State but one has been on the CFR or the Trilateral Commission (the Trilateral Commission was founded in 1973 by David Rockefeller and Zbigniew Brzezinski to establish a new economic order), many U.S.

presidents have been appointed from the CFR (including George Bush and Bill Clinton), and the CIA has been under CFR control since it was created. House dominated much of President Woodrow Wilson's agenda while in office, and after his success in establishing the Federal Reserve, his international banking contacts through various institutions in New York made him a key player in the early days of the CFR.

But the real power that brought the CFR into existence was in Britain. The Round Table sought to extend its influence into America and the CFR was its public face. It drew its financing from J.P. Morgan and Company, John Rockefeller, Otto Kahn, Jacob Schiff, Paul Warburg, and various tax exempt foundations, and though it presented itself as concerned with the status of the U.S., by 1936 its official handbook was openly declaring its intention to dominate international affairs. What is important to note here is that its origins were not American but British, and that it was this same elite group who were behind the League of Nations and the Federal Reserve. The ultimate aim was and always has been a single world government. This was acknowledged by CFR member and former Judge Advocate General of the U.S. Navy, Admiral Chester Ward, in his 1975 book "Kissinger And The Couch" he stated "The CFR has a goal of submergence of U.S. sovereignty and national independence into an all-powerful one-world government."

The consequences for the whole world of CFR influence have been devastating. Earlier we looked at some for the facts surrounding the arms trade: it is the CFR that has ensured that the U.S. is in an almost perpetual state of war. Ninety-three percent of the time the U.S. has been in existence it has been at war. Defence contractors such as Lockheed, Boeing and General Electric have had key members in the CFR and have benefited in trillions of dollars in profits. World War I was also a useful way of raising the idea of a one-world government as a solution to international conflicts. The League of Nations had been the hope of this global plan, but the U.S. Senate was so unimpressed with the Treaty of Versailles that House and his fellow CFR members would have to find another route to their goal: one feature of this was the recognition of the need to change public opinion.

The CFR offers vast sums in academic endowments to ensure scholars and universities present their narrative, and leading academics are only too aware that to challenge the CFR world view means an end to their careers. And so graduates are being produced who are indoctrinated with the belief that a single global consciousness is needed to meet the problems faced by humanity. The CFR has been at the centre of the promotion of the switch to digital money, and CFR voices have championed the concept of global population danger and the need for greater access to abortion as a means of control.

It was the expansion of national corporations into international monopolies that has provided the CFR with both the need for greater international control to protect their business interests, but also the means by which to gain this control. Through their universal control of financial institutions, the elite are able to orchestrate banking crises through which they can make unimaginable profits. For example, in 1929 Paul Warburg arranged for colleagues to withdraw funds from the stock exchange before the crash of 1929. With their cash intact they were then able to purchase companies at a fraction of their true cost, which enabled the wealthy elite to expand their own financial empires while the rest of the country lost out. This pattern has continued so that today the public are told by politicians that they must live with austerity while the gap between the rich and poor escalates. When President Franklin Roosevelt removed the U.S. dollar from the gold standard in 1934, the age of inflation caused by unrestrained growth in the supply of money meant that the only limit to the profits the bankers could make was how poor the public was willing to become. President Roosevelt is remembered for his "New deal" for America, which was really a programme of borrowing from the very institutions that had caused the depression in the first place.

The CFR has consistently lobbied for the United Nations to be given greater powers over national governments. This agenda is promoted by the CFR controlled media, including the Washington Post and Time Life Magazine. On the fiftieth anniversary of the CFR publication "Foreign Affairs", Kingman Brewster summed up this attitude towards the UN when he stated that national self-governance should be limited, so that countries "take some risks in order to invite others to pool their sovereignty with ours." (In his article "Reflections On Our National Purpose"). Slogans such as "world peace" and a "shared brotherhood" are presented to mask the true nature of the plan for the tyranny of a single world government. The academic, psychological and media resources at the disposal of the CFR ensure that ideas are gradually planted into the public consciousness so that when policy is revealed it finds an audience that is primed to receive it. Education is another tool in this process, and CFR member John Dewey saw the de-Christianising of America as an achievable goal under the slogan "atheism, socialism and evolution". This manufacturing of consent is considered "public enlightenment" by CFR insiders, and when President Nixon was guided into his massive bombing campaign on Cambodia by CFR member Henry Kissinger, it was felt the public did not even have to be informed. Other activities prompted by Kissinger, such as the support of the coup that put General Pinochet into power in Chile in 1973, the invasion of East Timor in 1975 by Indonesia that led to genocide, and the South African invasion of Angola in 1975, could be presented in whatever way was felt most appealing to the U.S. public who had no alternative sources of information other than the mainstream media. While U.S. politicians were being convinced that this level of ruthless military involvement in other nations' affairs was for the good of U.S. interests, the CFR used its vast military resources to further its own agenda, considering the national sovereignty of any individual state as an obstacle to eventually be overcome.

One of the recurring themes in CFR publications in recent decades has been to create a perception of human beings as a threat to the wellbeing of the planet. People are the problem, we are being told, and this is then linked with the idea that there are too many people for the world to sustain. In fact it is the high levels of consumption in North America and Western Europe that are a problem, but since the system of economics we are presented with requires national economies to constantly grow which requires mass consumerism, the CFR never highlights what might be the real issue. The false perception of world population growth has been reinforced by outrageous forecasts by the UN which have repeatedly been proven to be false.

But why would the CFR promote such ideas? One of the reasons is to change our view on abortion. The CFR has been behind a number of bills passed in the U.S. which increasingly liberalise abortion practice. In 1996 and 1998 Bill Clinton argued for partial-birth abortion, which involves the killing of infants as they emerge at birth. In 1997 Clinton gave hundreds of millions of dollars to international family planning groups that promoted abortion. A number of people who worked in Clinton's administration went on to find jobs with the RAND Corporation, which is a CFR think tank that promotes the need for population control. In the last few years The Open Society Institute, one of George Soros' tax exempt foundations, is issuing grants to groups working to promote abortion. This support for abortion groups goes beyond the debate of whether abortion should be legal, it forms part of the agenda for population reduction around the world. Agenda 21, which we mentioned earlier, has as one of its goals, not just a limit on the growth of human population, but a real reduction of present numbers. Birth control, abortion, compulsory sterilisation (such as the CIA carried out in villages in India in the 1950s) were considered the necessary tools for achieving this reduction, but have proved inadequate for the task. In the "Initiative For The United Nations, Eco '92

263

Earth Charter", we read: "The present vast over population, now far beyond the world carrying capacity, cannot be answered by future reductions in the birth rate due to contraception, sterilisation and abortion, but must be met in the present by the reduction in the number presently living."

Let us be clear, what is being proposed is the deliberate killing of many millions of people: perhaps we should not be surprised that the U.S. has a patent on the current strand of the Ebola virus. We should not be surprised at this because it is the inevitable conclusion of the green movement which identifies human beings as being a threat to mother earth. In "The First Global Revolution" we find the underlying philosophy, "All these dangers are caused by human intervention, and it is only through changed attitudes and behaviour that they can be overcome. The real enemy is humanity itself". The debate on global warming (now called climate change) is motivated by the intention to use the threat of environmental catastrophe as a means of manipulating the public into accepting what would otherwise be unacceptable. It has already begun with increases in taxes, the loss of certain basic rights and freedoms, and most importantly, the growing willingness to allow governments to take control over many more aspects of our lives. Global warming/climate change is one more means by which a world government will be established. When there is no longer any objection to the belief that climate change is produced by human behaviour, it will be possible to establish the idea that the only possible solution is a single entity overseeing all human activity on the planet. As stated by Christina Figureres, one of the key figures in the UN departments overseeing environmental issues, "global communism is the only solution to global warming". The threat of environmental disaster is presented as a universal threat, and so it becomes a natural step to recognise that we must abandon our individuality in favour of collective action. Already there are university scholars in the U.S. calling for legal action against those they are calling "climate change deniers": the same language that has enabled the German government to imprison historians who have dared question the statistics that are presented as part of the holocaust narrative.

The CFR's money can be linked to a number of programmes that hide behind buzzwords like "diversity" but when we look more closely we discover they create greater division and hostility between people. For example, the "Black Lives Matter" movement has created racial tension by by-passing debate and communication, and stirring people into protest and violent reprisal for the injustices its members feel have been done to them. Similarly feminist causes have been supported to pit one gender against another, and while the public is divided on itself the real masters of the game go unchallenged.

The Council On Foreign Relations is no more than an organisation of private citizens who have come together to protect and promote their own interests. But their level of wealth has given them access to government and influence over international policy that is entirely undemocratic. They meet with elected officials and no records are published of their discussions. The fact that the CFR is missing from news stories and never appears in the version of history taught in schools and universities testifies to the extent of its power. The CFR is more than a sign of Satan's kingdom; it is one of the most powerful weapons used against us. The greed and corruption that drives the CFR feeds on the wellbeing of ordinary people, degrading people's standard of living and even their sense of themselves. But the real target is Christianity. Over the next three chapters we will look specifically at how the Christian faith is the principle target of these movements, both directly and through the promotion of atheism.

Chapter 15 ~ Christianity The Real Enemy

While all Orthodox Christians understand that the use of war as a means of increasing personal wealth and the social injustices created by private banks, the promotion of abortion as a means of family planning, and all the other corrupt practices we have mentioned, are in conflict with the values of the Kingdom of God, we must now recognise that the war being waged is on Christ Himself. While the challenge to God's laws is a symptom of evil, it is Christ's Body, the Church, which is the real target of Satan's plan.

There was a surprising amount of media coverage when the owners of Masterpiece Cakeshop in Colorado were prosecuted for refusing to make a cake for a same sex wedding. The owners felt that to do so would endorse something which was in conflict with their Christian beliefs. They were threatened with up to twelve months imprisonment after the Colorado Attorney General filed a complaint against them on the grounds that they had discriminated against the two gay men. Media pundits chose to discuss the case in terms of whether someone's religious convictions gave them the right to deny others a service available to the public: in effect denying them their human rights.

267

The cake shop owners lost the case, and so it was made clear in law that Christians could not refuse to participate in something they felt was morally wrong. In short, Christians will face prison if they refuse to sanction something that is in opposition to the Christian faith.

This was not an isolated incident. Senior Master Sergeant Philip Monk was serving at Lackland Air Force base and was concerned about an instructor who was being sanctioned for expressing his religious objections to homosexuality. Monk was then questioned about his own beliefs, and as a result was told he was in violation of U.S. Air Force policy because he revealed his Christian faith. Monk was relieved of his duties, despite having a flawless service record.

The Bank of Montreal, in Canada, is running a campaign against Christians. In March 2014 it wrote to the Law Society asking that accreditation be denied any colleges which did not reflect inclusiveness. In effect this means all Christian colleges will be excluded from training lawyers. The bank's vice president, Simon Fish, said that they would only do business with legal firms which not only support inclusiveness, but which have a work force which reflects diversity: they must be able to demonstrate a sufficient LGBT presence or else lose their custom. The bank has set up a group called Legal Leaders for Diversity to which most Canadian corporations have now signed up. The specific aim of the group is to promote the opportunities of LGBT lawyers, and so far the only group they have attacked is Christians.

In the U.K. discrimination against Christians has occurred in similar cases. Bed and breakfast owners, Peter and Hazel Bull, were fined for refusing to allow a gay couple to use one of their rooms. The Bulls had a policy of not allowing any unmarried couples to share a bed in their home, but the courts considered their actions an act of discrimination on the grounds of the couple's sexuality (no heterosexual couple had ever taken them to court). The Bulls were targeted as part of the ongoing attack on Christians by the LGBT community who use the law to establish the precedence of their rights over the rights of others.

A registrar working in Islington, North London also suffered the law's refusal to recognise the validity of her Christian faith. Lillian Ladele was sacked because when David Cameron's Conservative government introduced same sex marriage, she felt she could not conduct them. Rather than arrange for another registrar to conduct services for gay couples, Islington town hall got rid of her. This was a result of laws pushed forward under the previous Labour government by Harriet Harman, who we have already encountered with reference to her work alongside paedophile groups in the 1970s. Harman (a lawyer by trade) developed the Equity Act of 2010 which makes discrimination against Christians so easy. The freedom of anyone to follow their religious convictions has been removed to protect the rights of the gay community.

This is not an isolated example of government policy, but typical of what is happening in Britain today. When we listen to the BBC discuss the latest Islamist terrorist outrage, we should notice how reporters refer to the problem caused by "religion" and "religious extremists" rather than specifically Islamic terrorists. The goal is to establish a discourse in which religion itself is identified as the threat, a discourse controlled by different groups antagonistic to Christianity. The U.K. government has introduced a number of pieces of legislation intended to combat "extremism", most of which threaten the right to free speech in all religions. For example, Conservative MP Mark Spencer acknowledged that David Cameron's programme of "British Values" means that the focus on tolerance will quickly result in traditional Christian values becoming identified as extremism. If a priest or minister preaches on the topic of sexual morality, and refers to homosexual practices as evil, they may be in danger of being prosecuted for committing a hate crime. After the U.K. legalisation on gay marriages, Essex County Council sent a letter to all churches in the area instructing them that they must comply with the new legislation or else face legal action: the council had missed the detail about churches having exemption, but the action demonstrates the underlying intention to force Christians to comply with the new agenda.

British Values has become a key phrase in U.K. education. OFSTED inspectors can now fail schools during an inspection if they do not see evidence that these values are being taught. All U.K. teachers are now being trained to identify students who may be expressing extremist views. The problem is, neither the government nor those in education have properly understood the difference between someone who is an extremist and someone who holds what others might consider extreme views. A Muslim child insisting that women should have their faces covered in public is not an extremist because of these views, however objectionable many might find them. Similarly, a Christian child arguing in class that homosexuality is wrong is expressing traditional Christian values, and should not be branded as intolerant. It is a very peculiar interpretation of the word "tolerance" which requires everyone to adopt a single moral view, and which enables gay rights to supersede any and all other rights. It is a form of tolerance where only the liberal humanistic views of those in power will be tolerated.

While working in a school I had been teaching at for twelve years, I was required to attend a meeting with the head teacher. He had gone through my

Facebook account and found a link I had clicked on six months before which he said was expressing extremist views. The link was to a video of an Orthodox Christian monk talking about the suffering of the Palestinians during Israeli bombing raids. When I began to explain why I thought this was a legitimate position to hold, I was told that this particular video wasn't the problem. In another video the monk had made he expressed the Christian view on homosexuality, and this was why I was being warned. It was this experience that made me realise I had to leave teaching.

We have entered a stage where any public expression of faith can be interpreted as extreme. In Wales the Labour led government has adopted the anti-extremist philosophy so completely that it has proposed removing all religious education from schools in favour of "social cohesion" classes. This will further the culture which is now being established where open debate or questioning of certain assumptions will be utterly unacceptable. The outcome will inevitably be a situation where parents will be denied the right to teach their children their moral and religious views. There are already U.S. feminists arguing that parents who raise their children within a religious faith are committing child abuse. Let us look further at this issue by considering the situation in France and the U.S., two countries which outwardly appear to have very different cultures, but in which we find the same anti-Christian forces at work.

Since 1905 French law has determined that church and state should remain separate. It is illegal for any local or national government body to promote any religious dogma, supposedly including atheism. This means that anyone working in an official capacity for the state must not even wear any overtly religious symbols. While this was the legal situation, a relaxed approach was taken up to the 1990s about Christian students wearing crosses or Jewish boys wearing a kippah. With the rise in the number of Muslim immigrants, French feminist writers began to argue that Muslim girls must not be permitted to wear head scarves because they represent a form of female oppression. This opposition was reinforced when France became the target of a number of Islamic terrorist attacks, and many French people began to view head scarves as an unacceptable sign of the Muslim presence. This came to a head in 1989 when three girls were expelled from a school in Creil, outside Paris, for refusing to remove their scarves. There was a great deal of public discussion on the matter which resulted in the government having to act. In 2004 Jacques Chirac passed a bill which outlawed anything in schools which demonstrated affiliation to any religious belief. All crosses had to be removed from classrooms and from the necks of students and teachers.

What we see here is the use of political arguments, particularly feminism and ideas about what French culture should stand for, alongside the changes brought about by increasing pluralism. As atheists can argue that Christianity is now just one faith amongst many, any laws applied to other faiths must also apply to Christianity. With so much attention focussed on Islamic extremists, the measures taken in reaction to their activities and the consequences to a nation's culture are always directed at Christianity too: since to not do so would be discriminative. Once more we encounter an example of the new language, full of positive sounding terms and presented as protecting the vulnerable, being used as a weapon against the Church.

A separation of state and church is also maintained in the U.S.A., but for different reasons to those in France, however, we see there the same anti-Christian agenda at work. In the U.S. there was a strong anti-Roman Catholic feeling amongst many who had fled from Europe. We find the first hints of what was to come in 1870 when the Ohio Supreme Court upheld a resolution banning Bible readings from school lessons. In the U.S. schools became the focus for a number of different arguments, including immigration and the pluralism within the Christian denominations. As a means of overcoming some of these disputes, many schools began to teach the Bible from the same

274

perspective as any other piece of literature: this opened the door for the secularisation of the treatment of the Holy Scriptures, something which developed over the following years.

In June of 1962 the United States Supreme Court declared that a prayer that had been approved by the New York Board of Regents for use in schools was a violation of the First Amendment. The court decided that the use of such a prayer constituted an establishment of religion, and less than a year later they applied the ruling to Bible readings in schools in Abington. The Supreme Court's decisions were heavily influenced by the pronouncements and decisions made in the nineteenth century but set the path for what was to follow. The California Senate Bill 1146 is the latest consequence. It seeks to abolish religious exemptions in the rules governing the appointment of teachers in colleges and schools. This means that a Christian establishment will not be able to seek to appoint staff who share the school's religious faith. In effect, it will abolish all Christian higher education in California. The bill also targets any institution which combines religious teaching with education, something which some parents and students specifically choose.

The bill was created as a result of an LGBT focus on colleges and universities that have a religious ethos. LGBT activists focussed on the exemptions granted to these colleges which require other colleges to provide androgynous toilets and showers and other amenities which LGBT groups insist must not be gender specific. But LGBT groups have an objection which goes beyond who can use particular toilets, they insisted that all religious teaching is a form of discrimination and should therefore be banned. Of the two hundred and eighty-one university options in California, only forty-two are religious in nature. The LGBT community has enough options not to have to attend an institution which has practices that offend them, but personal offence is not the real issue. By changing the law in this way they hope to enable future law suits to be made in civil courts against religious educational establishments, which will lead to their closure.

One single case highlights where we have arrived. Ryan Rotela, a student at Florida Atlantic University, was required as part of a lesson to write Christ's name on a piece of paper and stamp on it. When he refused his professor, Deandre Poole, decided to have him sanctioned. Only when local Christians protested against what was happening did the President for Student Affairs, Charles Brown, apologise for what had happened. Poole was forced to take leave but kept his job. Such a story would have been unthinkable only a few years ago, but the liberal atmosphere that permeates our colleges and universities has become emboldened in its attitude towards Christianity.

We are witnessing an acceleration in the attack on Christianity as the occult slips further into the centre of what is perceived as ordinary life by most people. New Age ideas have become so mainstream that many practitioners do not even think they are doing anything occult at all. The success of Freemasonry has been to present its beliefs in such a way as to separate them from their true sources and nature. Few know that the founders of both the Mormons, John Smith, and of the Jehovah's Witnesses, Charles Taze Russell, were Masons and that their cults are a deliberate attempt to mislead and confuse. Many Oriental occult healing, meditation and yoga practices have found their way into other Christian communities too, seen as scientific, or accepted just because they get results. When yoga was first introduced into the U.K. it was with the slogan "There is no yoga without Hinduism, and there is no Hinduism without Yoga". But this presentation has been dropped, and westerners have been convinced that it is a spiritually neutral set of exercises. Even something as apparently benign as homeopathy was founded by the German Freemason Hahnemann who read widely on the occult. With so many people now opening their lives to demonic influences, it is no wonder that we are witnessing such a rapid decline in the morality and very nature of our culture.

All of this is happening by design. In 1922 Alice Bailey wrote in "Initiation: Human And Solar": "Very definitely may the assurance be given here that, prior to the coming of the Christ, adjustments will be made so that at the head of all great organisations will be found either a master, or an initiate who has taken the third initiation. At the head of certain great occult groups, of the Freemasons of the world, and of the various great divisions of the church, and resident in many of the great nations will be found initiates or masters."

Our lives are being rearranged in more personal ways too: marriage and the family unit are key targets, as they have always been for the Babylonian Mysteries. The sanctity of marriage is undermined by films, television and modern literature, but the intention is also to divide children from their parents. At a time when many working people cannot survive on a single wage, the U.K. government has chosen to spend millions of pounds, not supplementing low wages, but to provide child care so that mothers can work too. The basic bond between parent and child is thus weakened as the focus becomes far more about the parenting role of the state and the degree to which it can be involved in bringing up our children. It has always been understood that raising children within the Christian faith requires that bond to be strong, and so we are being burdened with debt and longer working hours in order to keep us occupied with something other than our children.

Much of this is often characterised as a kind of war on faith, but it is only the beginning. We must see these examples as part of a process, not the whole event. In the rest of the world Christians suffer much more brutal persecution. The International Society for Human Rights, based in Frankfurt, states that eighty percent of all religious persecution in the world is suffered by Christians. Christians are now persecuted through imprisonment, torture and death in seventy-five percent of the countries on earth. One reason for this may be that Christian communities are often unwilling to seek revenge and so may be perceived as easy targets. But this does not account for most of the cases since in the worst offending countries persecution is government-led and justified by law. Various independent agencies put the average number of Christian martyrs at ten thousand annually (though some estimates are much higher than this) and the figure is rising with each year.

There are sixty-five churches in Baghdad, and since the U.S. led invasion of Iraq, forty of them have been bombed. The Christian population has shrunk in Iraq since the second Gulf war from one and a half million to less than half a million. Saddam Hussein was a tyrant, but he prevented Islamic extremists from attacking Christian villages, which they are now free to do.

As bad as the situation now is in Iraq for Christians and other religious minorities, it only comes ninth in the list of most dangerous countries in which to be a Christian. In order of severity, the list is:

North Korea
Afghanistan
Saudi Arabia
Somalia
Iran
Maldives
Uzbekistan
Yemen
Iraq
Pakistan

In a number of these countries the principle cause of persecution is Islam, but this is not the only cause. In India, for example, extremist Hindus butchered over five hundred Christians in a single day in 2008. But at the top of the list is North Korea where it is estimated that at any one time there are over fifty thousand Christians imprisoned in labour camps, and since 1953 it is believed that more than three hundred thousand Christians have disappeared. The reason for this persecution is the Christian refusal to participate in the national cult of the secular leader, and so they are identified as enemies of the state. It is also worth noting that the U.K. and U.S. have close links with Saudi Arabia, making huge arms deals with the royal family, and so turning a blind eye to the suffering of Christians there.

Western MSM is silent over this assault on Christians, which we may interpret in a number of ways. If we are trying to be generous, we might suppose that liberal humanists are focussed on what they perceive as a Christian aspect of past colonialism, and so are unable to recognise the reality for Christians today. But such a collective blind spot seems unlikely. We are left to conclude that western journalists do not wish to report the persecution of Christians because they either do not consider it newsworthy (since it is unimportant) or because they approve of it.

If any of this feels exaggerated, then Christians must ask themselves simple questions. Do we really believe that we are part of a spiritual war? Do we believe that there are demonic forces at work against us? It should not be so difficult to recognise that many people have willingly given themselves, knowingly or unknowingly, to the army that stands in opposition to Christ. But let us be clear, many people do so believing they are doing good. There were even some Communists who genuinely believed that by irradiating all signs of the Church from Russia they were freeing their countrymen from an unnecessary yoke. There are many LGBT people who genuinely believe that by promoting gay rights and being in opposition to any organisation that stands in their way will bring about greater liberty and justice. But no matter how sincerely someone believes something; such depth of feeling does not make it true. The world is working to convince us that freedom means being able to fulfil every desire and passion we may have. But Christianity tells us that such a way of life is slavery. Many who fight for the promotion of individual rights do so because they have no vision of anything beyond this world, and they have no sense of good and evil. But there is another group of people who fight the Church because they have consciously chosen to serve Satan. Let us be absolutely clear on this, just as we know and seek to serve Christ, there are powerful men and women who have given their allegiance to Lucifer. The changes we are witnessing in the world are moving in one direction because that is where they are being guided. We will be told time and again that it is all a matter of evolution, that our cultures and societies are naturally growing where they will, but as the likes of Alice Bailey revealed, it is working to a plan.

Chapter 16 ~ Evolution

It is arguable that no idea has had a greater impact on the world view of modern man than Darwin's theory of evolution. Darwin claimed that the biblical account of creation was contradicted by almost every aspect of the natural world, and he believed that he was able to offer an alternative explanation for man's existence to the one offered by Christianity. As a school teacher, I witnessed a growing acceptance amongst children of the theory of evolution as a scientific fact, but when questioned, few of them knew even the basic concepts that underpin it. When pushed, many people will say they believe "we came from monkeys", as though this somehow answers the question of what produced human beings, while usually having no idea of what Darwin actually proposed. Here we shall briefly summarise Darwin's ideas before identifying why they fail in the face of the scientific evidence. But this chapter is concerned with more than the failings of Darwinism; we will look at exactly why the theory is promoted, how it fits into the satanic agenda, and the inevitable consequences it produces.

Darwin's theory proposes that all living creatures have a common ancestry that we all came from the same primitive source and that through a gradual process of change we have the many types of animals that exist today. Darwin was clear that for this theory to be true, there must have been a gradual evolution without any sudden changes or discontinuities. Darwin believed that the process of change was driven by something called natural selection which he argued explained the directional and adaptive changes he claimed he had identified. In effect, the mechanism for change is nature eliminating inferior examples of a species, something the philosopher Herbert Spencer later described as "survival of the fittest". We must remember that Darwin was completely unaware of the existence of genes and DNA, and a number of questions have arisen in this field which we shall consider. In short, Darwinism claims that the diversity of life is explained by adaptation to environment and the selection of mates according to their strength, or speed, or whatever else is likely to make offspring more successful.

This single paragraph is, of course, a very brief summary, but it communicates the basic ideas that underpin his theory. For many people I encounter, the false belief that science is in opposition to faith is often rooted in a suspicion that Darwin managed to provide an explanation of why life is as it is without the need to involve God. So let us consider the problems with Darwin's theory, and why it contradicts the evidence.

The most obvious reason we can be sure Darwinism isn't true is that the fossil records tell us otherwise. About five hundred and thirty million years ago there was an event (a relatively brief period of time in geological terms of five to ten million years) called the Cambrian Explosion. This is when we see the sudden emergence of different animal types with eyes, nervous systems, spinal cords and other features, which have no precursors in the fossil record. Darwin was well aware of this event; he described it as deeply troubling, and admitted that if such an explosion or radiation of animal types were true it would undermine his whole theory. But he explained it away by believing that one day enough fossils would be unearthed that demonstrated links to previous animals, and so support his idea of a gradual change from a common ancestry. Here we see Darwin discovering scientific evidence which contradicted his theory, but rather than change his ideas, he proposed that the fossil record was incomplete: something which he believed would be rectified by future palaeontologists. However, over the next hundred years, with teams of palaeontologists searching for the evidence which would inevitably make their name in the scientific community, no such evidence has ever been found.

Believers in Darwinism were then forced to adopt a different argument. They claimed that the reason the fossils supporting gradual evolution before the

Cambrian event do not exist is because the conditions were not right back then to preserve soft-bodied creatures. But once more the scientific evidence contradicts this claim. Pre-Cambrian fossils of soft tissue have been found, including the delicate embryos of sponges: if these were capable of being fossilised then Darwin's evidence most certainly could have been if it ever existed. Writing about the sudden appearance of these animals Richard Dawkins said "it is as though they were just placed there without any evolutionary history." The problem has become more acute for Darwinians as more fossils are found: the time period during which the Cambrian event occurred is shrinking, and the evolutionary explanation becomes even more ridiculous. Ninety percent of the earth's geological history occurred before the Cambrian period, and yet there is not a single piece of fossil evidence to support the idea that the animals that emerged at this time had any evolutionary link with their predecessors: Darwinism requires that we find transitional forms, but they don't exist. And furthermore we do not find fossils of the many evolutionary dead ends and trials which would have been needed to produce what came into being.

Darwin's key error was to fail to recognise that the categories or groups of animal types came into existence at the same time. During the Cambrian event these animal types, called phyla, such as vertebrates, arthropods, echinoderms and so on, emerge with their key features which make them distinct from one another. The common ancestry idea is nonsense when we understand that this distinction between phyla remains regardless of variation with animal groups. In other words, animals may change within their group, but they never move from one to another, they do not share an earlier beginning. Darwinism also states that over time more animal groups must emerge as species evolve and become more complex. But again, the evidence contradicts this assumption, since almost all phyla that exist today came into being at the Cambrian event.

Darwin admitted that the fossil evidence perplexed him; he said it was "inexplicable", but seemed to honestly believe that one day the evidence would be found to prove him right. Darwinists today, however, are fully aware of what evidence has been found, and we can only wonder at the scientific honesty missing from so many academic institutions that withdraw funding from research which dares to challenge the prevailing paradigm. Children are never taught in school about the actual fossil evidence, but this may be partly due to their science teachers not knowing about it themselves. Most contemporary palaeontologists have acknowledged that they do not believe the fossils Darwin believed existed will ever surface.

As mentioned earlier, Darwin was not aware of the existence of DNA, and the fact that for the Cambrian event to have taken place the new genetic material must have come from somewhere. Mutations in DNA cannot account for the sudden changes we observe, particularly the emergence on such a huge scale of new phyla. In fact, some geneticists are now pointing out that random selection and natural selection are simply incapable of producing the emergence of a single animal group in such a short period of time, let alone almost all of the phyla still in existence today.

A further difficulty for evolutionary theory is the issue of homosexuality. It is something of a curiosity for geneticists that the claim that people are born gay suggests a genetic component. However, the persistence of male homosexuality over evolutionary time raises the problem of how the gene could be surviving if homosexuals are not producing offspring. The biologists are caught between a rock and a hard place, since the political climate will not permit them to suggest there can be no genetic cause of homosexuality. U.S. studies have shown that only thirty-seven percent of homosexuals have a child, which would result in a reduction in the number of homosexuals over time, but in fact the numbers are increasing. Similarly, it is known that if a homosexual has an identical twin, there is only a twenty percent chance of them both being gay.

But the discovery of genetics resulted in a far more important issue for Darwinists. In the 1970s biologists found that the majority of DNA does not appear to serve an obvious purpose, it became known as "Junk DNA". Darwinists such as Dawkins leapt at the discovery, claiming that it was clear evidence that our genome contains evidence of the trials and errors of evolution. However, recent research has shown that what is called non-coding DNA does have a function, and as the understanding of DNA grows, Darwinists have quickly dropped the term "Junk DNA" from their papers. But not before their evolutionary assumptions about DNA resulted in decades where little research was carried out into non-coding DNA because the Darwinists had concluded that it performed no function and as Dawkins said, it is something akin to a parasite on the functioning DNA. The Darwinian paradigm resulted in research not taking place, delaying the recognition of the regulatory functions of this "junk".

Darwin's theories face further difficulties. While his theory attempts to explain a process of change, it offers nothing to account for how life began in the first place. Media commentators will often refer to life beginning in some primordial sludge, but it all becomes rather vague when the question is put how something that was not alive became alive. Life cannot come into existence from non-life through chemical processes: biologists have tried very hard to achieve this. But neither does Darwinism satisfy the question of how life that existed as a few molecules was transformed into us. The fossil record gives no explanation of how this happened. Furthermore, human beings have many abilities and traits which have no survival value at all, such the capacity to appreciate aesthetics or reflect on philosophical and religious questions, and many of these qualities are valued as what distinguishes us as truly human: they are not minor, peripheral features.

Darwin argued that from simple, basic life, response to environment led animals to become more complex. But the basic idea of entropy is that in any closed system, which life on earth is, things do not become more complex, but break down, moving from order to disorder. Without the involvement of an intelligent agent, the system moves to chaos.

The U.S. philosopher Jerry Fodor describes survival of the fittest as a circular argument. He points out that it is only "survival of those who survive", since the fittest are by definition those who survived. He argues that there are many traits that we have that have nothing to do with survival, but are passed on through our genes, but which certainly have nothing to do with us being the fittest. It is only the reasoning observer who later determines that survival can be attributed to particular inherited qualities. This leads us to the issue of altruism. Darwinists claim that it is the survival of our species that is paramount, and that this explains why we would make self-sacrifices for others. But there is a real problem with this argument, since it suggests that when we act for the benefits of others at our own expense we are merely responding to a genetic impulse. Therefore, to be truly free in the sense of making independent conscious choices, we would have to act in an utterly selfish and unsocial way. In fact, the more extreme our anti-social behaviour, the more free we would be. Certainly the likes of Aleister Crowley would wholeheartedly agree with this line of argument, but as Christians we recognise it as a corruption of truth.

There are many truths for which scientific research is an unsuitable tool. We know and accept much of human history on the basis of personal accounts, documentation and eye witness reports. When it comes to the nature of our existence, the events being explored can never be repeated in an experiment, scientists can only reflect on the evidence of what is present now. Creation is not something science can properly investigate because it cannot reproduce it as an experiment. We do, however, have documented accounts of people who claim to have interacted directly with the Creator, many more examples than for other historical events over which there is little argument. But Darwinism is more than a genuine desire to find the truth of how we came to exist; it is a deliberate attempt to deny God. Anyone who claims to be a Christian evolutionist has failed to understand one of the parts of that term, since they are mutually incompatible. Evolution is an atheistic ideology which allows for no participation of God. It proposes that life automatically moves towards greater perfection, that what went before is inferior to the present and what is to come. This is the false philosophy that has been implanted into modern man's perception; it is sustained by an illusion of technology which masks the real decline in man's soul. Millions sit vacantly in front of the mindless garbage broadcast on television, while few today could hope to read and understand a novel by Dickens. But this was the literature of the common people a hundred and fifty years ago, who were capable of sitting quietly and reading and reflecting on such works. We see a moral decline where what was once known to be sinful is celebrated and anyone who questions the change is targeted as evil. We see and know that this is not a move to greater perfection, and Orthodox Christians have been warned many times by the saints that we in this age are spiritual pigmies compared with those who went before us. Our culture is confused and dangerous, it is rapidly moving to greater imperfection, while proclaiming itself the best there has ever been. In a world where we consider those from the past inferior to us, then their teachings and wisdom must also be inferior. Evolutionary thinking enables man to cut himself off from tradition since all that is new transcends what went before, and we are left lost on an ocean of ideas without a rudder. The New Age movement is an inevitable result of these false ideas, and are developed at length in the writings of Teilhard de Chardin, a Jesuit priest who participated in the Piltdown Man hoax in order to further promote his theories: long after the hoax was discovered his ideas persist.

Dawkins stated that "Even if there were no actual evidence in favour of the Darwinian Theory, we should still be justified in preferring it over all rival theories." Dawkins is revealing his and many other academics' first concern, which is the denial of God. He uses the word "justified" because of his personal loathing of Christianity. The powerful elites are promoting the theory of evolution because it supports their plan. First it undermines the common man's understanding of himself as a child of God, and seems to provide good, scientific reasons for doing so. But it also enables what is to come. Once we have accepted that it is only natural for the fittest to survive at the expense of the weak, we must ask ourselves who are the strong and weak? The globalists consider themselves at the very point of the pyramid, while the great majority are beneath them. The super-rich want nothing more than to justify their lifestyle in naturalistic terms that remove the need for guilt over injustice. And in a world where overpopulation is seen to be a threat to our continuation, then the answer is to remove the threat. How completely logical it is for the elites to want the elimination of those who compete with them for resources. And since man has been conditioned to see himself as no more than any other animal on earth with no greater intrinsic value, what crime or tragedy is being committed when the fittest do what they must to protect themselves? Social Darwinism means mass genocide, and if you are willing to accept the survival of the fittest, you are embracing a terrible future for us all.

Chapter 17 ~ Nihilism And Materialism

The Theory of Evolution has been championed by many because it satisfies a desire to undermine and eventually eradicate faith from public life. But it is only one strand in a philosophical and political rope that it is hoped will form the noose around Christianity's neck. The popular understanding of these ideas is that they belong to their particular areas of study and are independent of one another. For example, most people are raised to believe that Darwinism is a product of scientific research, and will stand or fall according to whatever evidence is found. But as we have seen, this is not the case, evolutionary theory flies in the face of paleontological discoveries, because those who believe in it will protect it in the face of all scientific evidence. Similarly, there are political ideas which present themselves as being about the search for the most just ways of organising society, but are in reality an expression of atheism. In particular, we will see how materialism and nihilism are the driving forces behind different modern political stances, and that without these atheistic philosophies there could be no communism or the LGBT movement.

Communism is often perceived as a more extreme form of socialism, and since in the U.K. and other countries, there are a number of people who describe themselves as Christian socialists; communism is seen as one more political opinion amongst many. It is often associated with themes that may even appear Christian, such as concern for the poor and a distrust of extreme wealth. Marxist ideas have penetrated deeply into western thinking, however, it is impossible to be both a Christian and a communist; the two belief systems are utterly opposed.

Communism has at its core a belief that the universe has no spiritual component: only physical matter is real, and anything that appears to be spiritual in nature is really only a product of matter. Communism maintains that all progress results from conflict, and that the changes needed to improve human life can only be achieved through social conflict. Communists believe that the true foundation of all human life is economics, and everything else, such as art, ethics, religion and the illusion of love, are just a consequence of economic conditions.

This brutal form of materialism is opposed to Christianity, not just because the latter maintains the importance of the spiritual nature of life, but because the two present opposing concepts of man himself. For Christians, our ultimate value comes from having been created in the image of God. Christianity teaches that every human being is distinct and of immeasurable worth. Communism draws on Darwinism and teaches that it is man's intellect alone which distinguishes him from other animals, and so the worth of a person is found in their capacity to reason and contribute economically.

Communism is not only dangerous because of its power as a philosophical position, but also in the consequences it has on those societies based on it. Communism denies the fallen nature of man, and so requires no limits to his morality. Furthermore, Communism abolishes the right of the individual to have rights over his relationship with others: all of us become a part of the state to which all ultimate rights are handed. The rights we might take for granted become subordinated to that of the larger body: exactly what we see in UN agenda. Through policies which are portrayed as responding to global threats, and so entirely necessary, the UN is seeking to deprive us of fundamental freedoms relating to possessions and lifestyle, in order to serve the global economy.

This degradation of the human person must be established as a general mind-set if the agenda of Antichrist is to be furthered. We already see one in ten babies conceived in the U.K. being aborted, a clear indication that the public view of human life has been altered. Dr. Bernard Nathanson, a defender of abortion in the U.S., stated that during the seventy years in which the U.S.S.R. was controlled by the communists, there were on average sixteen million abortions every year. The

Manifesto of the U.S. Communist Party begins with the statement that one of its objectives is the "abolition of the family". Children are to lose the fundamental relationship with their parents so that they can be transformed into instruments of labour serving the greater economic need. From this perspective, it is only natural that unwanted economic units may be disposed of without troubling anyone's conscience.

Communism is also opposed to Christianity because of its understanding of the purpose of science. There are many Christians working in biology and physics who see their role as discovering something of the mystery of creation through the material world. Communism understands science as being produced from man's struggle to overcome nature. Communism proclaims that the physical universe is eternal, it is matter itself which will never end, and talk of soul or spirit is rejected. Therefore we have no eternal or ultimate value as human beings, and any feelings to the contrary are dismissed as emotionalism.

What is not made clear within the contemporary political and social discourse is that feminism is not only based in the writings of Marx, very often feminist writers repeat verbatim what he espoused. But traditional, liberal feminists have found the ground moving beneath their feet, and writers such as Germain Greer, once the darling of feminist commentators, are now considered outdated, and part of the problem, by LGBT spokesmen. This is because of the growth of nihilism.

In order to strip human life of meaning, simply distracting us with entertainments, scaring us with environmental and terrorist threats or dangling material rewards before us, will only achieve so much. There will always remain enough people who reflect on their purpose and meaning that a satisfactory philosophical system is needed to underpin the kingdom of Antichrist: that system is nihilism.

Nihilism grew out of the increasingly secular culture of nineteenth century Europe where belief in God was being attacked in many different ways. The title itself comes from the Latin word nihil meaning nothing, and the Greek suffix ism. As man grew proud of his new scientific discoveries it was concluded by some that the whole universe could be explained by the empirical method, and everything reduced to what is observable. This laid the foundations of communism. As early as 1855 Nikolai Chernyshevsky was arguing that all aesthetics, human freedom and even human individuality and distinctiveness was an illusion. This of course, had enormous consequences for ethics, as it freed philosophers to imagine a world where there is no eternal consequence for anything we choose to do.

The name most associated with nihilism is Friedrich Nietzsche (1844-1900). But in

Nietzsche's writings the term nihilism often means Buddhism, a life of renunciation of material concerns, and he saw this as a denial of life. However, as much as Nietzsche has been misunderstood in the popular mind, his real legacy was to identify an absence or denial of values, what he called "the end of metaphysics". By the time people like Albert Camus were writing in the mid-1950s, nihilism had become so established that it resulted in what Camus recognised as a meaninglessness, a nonsense, in his terms, "the absurd". Camus understood that there is within the man who chooses nihilism a contradiction, because however meaningless he may proclaim life, he will always value life over death. Modern biologists have dismissed this as a common feature of any living animal, an instinctive drive to survive. But Camus' point is greater than the biologists admit, it is recognition of the human heart's discomfort with the notion that everything can be reduced to an arbitrary notion, that every truth is relative, and that truth itself can be denied. Camus understood that the sense of meaningless that this produces is an unbearable condition: but of course, he wasn't living with fifty television channels and endless electrical gadgets to distract him.

Earlier I mentioned the link between the LGBT movement and nihilism. This is not a link that I have identified, but one made by its members. What we shall see is that the LGBT phenomenon is an inevitable outcome of the spread of nihilism. For LGBT writers, to claim the existence of norms of sexual identity is oppressive. In short, if we state that there are more heterosexual people than gay, we are making an oppressive statement. This is because LGBT claim that to consider their sexual preferences as being outside of a norm is offensive and an attempt to marginalise them. In order to prevent such attacks on them, their answer is to remove all distinctions between people because of their gender. Not only do they want us to consider everyone sexless, but the language we use must also reflect this. In universities across the U.S. and already a few in the U.K., students are being instructed to remove from their work all language that reflects gender since it is considered to be oppressive. LGBT writers argue that all normative categories with which we label people are unnatural, they do not exist in reality but are created through social discourse and language. If you think you are a particular race or gender, then you have adopted artificial constructs.

For Christians this is easily refutable. When we read the account of creation in Genesis we learn that God made species and types of creatures, but when it came to man He made them male and female. At the very beginning of creation God gave man an identity that was identifiable as male or female. We were not created like the other animals with a genderless, almost generic species called humanity, but with a gender that contributes to who and what we are.

But this is where the true essence of nihilism is identifiable. LGBT writers argue that it is not only the descriptions of the self which are artificial, but the very notion of us as individuals. The philosophy is developing so quickly that the aforementioned Germain Greer has been left behind. LGBT writers argue that to claim to be a woman (with rights etc.) is to engage with a system that is oppressive, and only by rejecting such categorisation can all people hope to be free. While head teachers proudly speak in assemblies about showing respect for LGBT people, few of them understand what it is they are speaking out in favour of. During my final year of teaching in 2016, not a single week passed without school management or students themselves raising the term LGBT. It was always in the context of equality and respect, as though it was simply an extension of the old feminist or gay movements. But the LGBT aim is the denial of all identity, a rejection of every and any form of classification or labelling.

The birth place of all the LGBT movement was Los Angeles, the city where the first gay pride parade took place in 1966 (when a twenty foot phallus was dragged through the streets). The LGBT movement identified three clear targets for their campaigning: the law, the mental health profession and the churches. Laws were relatively easy to change, since concepts of equality are readily espoused by politicians and those in the media. In 1973 homosexuality was officially removed from the list of pathologies treated by psychiatrists, and so LGBT attention moved to the churches. A direct assault failed, and so the strategy became one of building social pressure from outside the churches in order to make church goers feel they were being intolerant. While extremist LGBT members have disrupted church services, the media has supported the charge of bigotry against many traditional believers, keenly led by many Jewish groups (though there is no such support for LGBT in Israel). It is worth remembering that occult representations of Satan represent him as androgynous, possessing both male and female sexual organs.

As a result we have seen a growing acceptance of LGBT in the West, and similarly universal acceptance of same-sex marriage. The difficulty over gay marriage has been that the groups in favour and those opposed are arguing about entirely different subjects. Pro voices see the matter as an extension of marriage, one of equality, while those against reject what they see as a completely new redefinition of marriage. With the aim clearly set as one of destruction of the family, we can see how the undermining of the meaning of marriage will help reach it. Same sex marriage is a separation of our present culture with what has gone before. It is liberation from the past for those in favour, and for secularists, all change is improvement. The evolutionary thinking convinces atheists that our society is forever overcoming the errors of the past, that all change is progress: but they fail to see that it is really decay. Man has simply taken all authority for himself, and nihilism tells him that even if he is wrong, what does it matter? Just a few decades ago even Americans knew that certain sexual practices are deviant, and that sex is not just a matter of personal choice. But today the U.S. is promoting homosexuality around the world, and all dissent is suppressed by labelling dissenters as bigots. Seeing themselves as nothing more than intelligent animals, modern men no longer have any restraint over their behaviour because morality is something people made up a long time ago. For now there is still some behaviour that is restricted on the grounds that it causes suffering to others, but this will pass. A future is coming when all men will be free to enjoy whatever their wallets permit, which will mean the very rich will openly do as they please. For now they must pretend, hide their activities behind false news stories and an illusion of being on our side: this will change.

Chapter 18 ~ Preparing For What Is To Come

The information presented in this book describes a plan that is satanic and active. It is clear that Satan is destroying the values and morality of our society. Faith is being painted in unattractive colours, so that it does not seem to offer the answers for which people are looking. Family bonds are being broken; marriage is being reinterpreted as no more than a legal contract or a romantic option. Human identity is being portrayed as a matter of choice and selection, and the distinctiveness of humanity is being dissolved in theories of evolution and existentialism. Our minds are becoming programmed by endless hours of digital information, and education is failing to provide the tools with which we can defend our capacity to think. Environmentalists are convincing a whole generation that people are the real problem, and that a solution must be found to kerb the expansion of human life. But it should come as no surprise to Christians who were warned by Christ to remain watchful for these things. If we are able to step back from the pressure and effects of our education and the various worldly voices, we may find a clarity of judgement that enables us to see what is behind these events. There will be rational, "sensible" people telling us that such things are far-fetched, that we must not speak of them since such talk will only upset people. Nearing the end of writing this book I began to wonder if I dared publish such ideas; I began to doubt the wisdom of risking the inevitable anger it would provoke. However, in May 2017 I made a visit to Mount Athos and had the opportunity of discussing some of these themes with a monk there. Not only did he encourage me to be confident about the reality of what is taking place, he provided me with further articles that extended my understanding of what is happening.

As Christians we try to maintain our focus on the world which is to come, but too often the world's portrayal of reality can weaken our grip on truth. We may doubt or even reject the idea that such evil is being committed in the world, since the newsreaders and politicians always present themselves in such reasonable and polite ways. But if we believe in Christ and the message of the Gospel, we know we are participating in a spiritual war, and that our enemy the devil will use any and every means of defeating us. We are living in a time of great apostasy and religious confusion. The deliberate denial of revealed truth has led many millions of people to turn their backs on God: we live in the very time that Christ warned us about when "the love of many shall grow cold" (Mt 24 v 12). The Gospel is no longer the centre of our culture; we see the Christian faith withdrawing from public life and being relegated to a private matter. We are living in a time when the world is clearly preparing for the coming of Antichrist: whether this will be in two, three or more generations, none of us can say. But there have been a number of prophetic voices warning of what is to come, and a number of these warn us of how close the final events now are. In this final chapter we will briefly remind ourselves of the biblical warnings before looking in detail at the more recent prophecies of Orthodox saints. We will then reflect on what this means for us now, and how we should respond.

Some will argue that there have always been Christians who have looked at the state of the world around them and interpreted it as a sign of the end of the world. But today, for the first time in human history, the world struggles with global threats: military technology that can obliterate almost all human life, there are claims of diminishing resources and potential environmental catastrophe, problems that are nothing like the world has faced before. We live in an age where digital financing has, for the first time, made a single world government possible. At the same time we can see a new religious consciousness forming, the New Age ideas that Father Seraphim Rose wrote about in the 1970s have been dramatically eclipsed by openness to satanic practices. And with an absence of Christian faith, the world is searching for man-made solutions that leave them vulnerable to the one who will seem to have all the answers.

For details about the end times in the New Testament we should look particularly at the twenty-fourth chapter of Mathew, the Book of Revelation, the second chapter of II Thessalonians and the third chapter of II Peter. In the Old Testament it is worth examining the Book of Daniel. The picture that emerges from these texts is of a world of wars, famines, earthquakes, false prophets, a false Christ and apostasy that will infect most people, even many in the Church. A time of great chaos and suffering will enable a leader to emerge who will solve the world's problems; he will bring peace and be adored by the majority of people on earth: he will then establish himself as Christ and rule from his throne in Jerusalem. Near the end, two Old Testament prophets who did not die, Elijah and Enoch, will return to convert many people back to Christ before the conclusion of time. The biblical assurance is that Antichrist will reign for no longer than three and a half years, and a number of saints have said that even this period will be cut short because of God's love of man. Finally these events will culminate in the return of Christ, the general resurrection of all who have died, and the final judgement where each will receive reward or punishment for their deeds. The order of these events is sometimes confused in our understanding but there have been clear indications from God's saints in how these things will come to pass and what to look for first. We will begin with prophecies from Russia from both before and after the establishment of the communist state. Then we will reflect on the words of more recent saints from Mount Athos and the guidance they offer us.

Amongst the ordinary people of Russia there is a spiritual reawakening, and this was foretold by a number of Russian saints as they warned of the coming atheistic persecution that was about to befall their nation. Long before 1917, God revealed that if the Russian people repented of their crimes (they were to commit regicide) they would experience a kind of rebirth, and would play an important role in the war with Satan through their defence of Orthodoxy. But these prophecies placed what we see happening at a specific point in the events to come. For example, Elder Barnabas of the Gethsemane Skete, who warned of the coming revolution, said: "persecutions against the faith will constantly increase. There will be unheard of grief and darkness, and almost all the churches will be closed. But when it will seem to people that it is impossible to endure it any longer, then deliverance will come. There will be a flowering. Churches will even begin to be built. But this will be a flowering before the end."

The terrible darkness that fell across Russia resulted in the deaths of tens of thousands of bishops, priests and monks, and the murder and imprisonment of many lay people. Elder Barnabas was right about the closing of churches, and also of the subsequent flowering of Orthodoxy. Many in Russia and elsewhere recognise the authentic voice of prophecy in his words, and so believe his warning that these things are a sign of the nearness of the end. Archbishop Theophan (the Recluse) considered the prophecies of Elder Barnabas and others as divine revelation, he said "I do not speak on my own, but give the revelation of the elders: the coming of Antichrist draws nigh and is very near."

Elder Ephraim of Arizona has stated that the Antichrist will not reveal himself until after a third world war. Other holy prophets have confirmed this, including Saint Paisios. But we should ask ourselves why so many will receive the false Christ and worship him. The first point we should note is that those who do not participate in the sacramental life of the Orthodox Church have no sense of the taste of authentic Christianity. They are vulnerable to falsehood since they have not participated in the Truth. But within the Church too there are many for whom their faith is merely an outward function, they do not seek to be transformed inwardly by God's grace. The life of spiritual struggle and self-sacrifice is becoming increasingly alien to the world, and all of us must guard ourselves against losing our saltiness. But more than this, the

Antichrist will at first not enforce his will on the world; he will come with words and actions that are full of apparent love and wisdom. He will present himself as the one who cares for us, who is able to unify all humanity, and those few Christians who reject him will be portrayed as evil. Persecution of the Church will follow the pattern we see already being established, where Christians are seen as bigots, as those unwilling to join together in worship with others of different faiths, as those unwilling to accept the freedoms the new forms of "liberation" offer: good and evil will have exchanged places in people's consciousness.

The Church in Russia faced a violent persecution and withstood every evil that was unleashed against it. But this was a church that had centuries of Christian life behind it, Orthodoxy was a natural part of their every-day life. We must ask ourselves how we are preparing for what is to come. In the West, the general practice is not to visit monasteries and holy elders, but to go to Disneyland and have "fulfilling experiences". How unprepared we are as a people, and how easy it will be to spiritually conquer us compared with the Russians. Saint Seraphim of Sarov warned that "In those days the remnant of the faithful are to experience in themselves something like that which was experienced once by the Lord Himself when He, hanging on a cross, felt Himself so forsaken by His Divinity, that He cried out "My God, why hast

Thou forsaken me?" The last Christians will experience in themselves a similar abandonment of humanity by the grace of God, but only for a short time." As Christ said, will He find faith on earth when He returns?

Amongst non-Orthodox Christians there is great confusion and heresy: they are ripe for the picking. Roman Catholicism has embraced many heresies and has stripped its rites of anything that could draw the faithful into an experience of God; it has allowed the fashion for innovation to turn its worship into a banal and empty ritual. Many Protestants have been taught the heresy of "millenarianism" (or "chiliasm"), which is the belief that Christ will physically reign on earth for a thousand years before the end of the world. This was condemned as heresy in the early Church, and comes from a misinterpretation of the Book of Revelation. The Church believes that the period of a thousand years in which Satan is bound is the present age. The Protestants have made two errors: they have interpreted the number one thousand as a literal period of time rather than recognising it as representing wholeness, and they have fallen into the same trap as those Jews who rejected Christ when he first came. The Pharisees and Scribes understood the Messiah to be a worldly ruler, they looked for God's Kingdom to be established as a military and political power on earth. Similarly the Protestants look for such an earthly reign at

Christ's second coming, an expectation which will only be fulfilled by Antichrist. The Jews who still profess to be waiting for the Messiah will also have their desires fulfilled by the man of iniquity. It does say in the Book of Revelation (8v1) that there will be silence in Heaven for a short space of time, and again some Protestants have mistaken this to point to this earthly rule of Christ. However, as Saint Paisios and others explained, this relates to a brief restoration of Orthodoxy (that may last as long as three generations) before the final terrible events take place. This confusion is no accident; the errors of doctrine will lead to an acceptance of Antichrist.

Let us now turn to the prophecies of Saint Paisios. He is particularly important because he is a saint who lived in modern times (he left this world in 1994) and so was able to discern the meaning of what is happening around us today. One recurring theme in his teaching is his concern over the lack of interest in what is happening, he called it a "mood of tranquillity". Saint Paisios recognised how the apocalyptic times we are living in are ignored even by many in the Church who prefer to seek a quiet life. He said that while "the minds of whole nations are in confusion" the enemies of Christ attack the Church by "quietly pulling out one stone after another." But he warned that even those who know only too well that this is happening remain silent. "Indifference is unacceptable", he said, a statement aimed at both the clergy and laity alike.

Saint Paisios understood the true nature of the satanic plan in our world, and said that "Today's situation can be resisted only spiritually, not by worldly means." In this he was consistent, repeatedly bringing people's attention back to what we must do to fight this battle. He taught that we must try to live simple, faithful lives, paying attention to our own condition before God. We must each recognise ourselves as a small corner of the Church, and work hard to protect that one piece. In this way, he said, we will collectively stand up to Satan. He did not call people to outlandish or overly dramatic responses, in fact he warned against this very thing. He said "Ours is an age of sensationalism and hullabaloo. But the spiritual life is not noisy." He recommended that Christians try to acquire a small piece of land in order to grow vegetables or keep chickens, so that when those who refuse to accept the mark of Antichrist in order to buy and sell, will at least have a little food.

Living in the 1990s, Saint Paisios saw clearly how far things had gone. He spoke out against the "Godlessness and blasphemy" which is shown on television, and declared that "The Old Testament Tower of Babel was child's play compared with our age." Reflecting on the Book of Revelation he said that much of what is described there is now beginning to surface, slowly transforming our world, and leading him to declare that "The world has turned into a madhouse," and that "we're on the verge of the end times."

Saint Paisios talked about many of the themes this book has touched on. Recognising how they are linked he said "Ecumenism, common markets, a one-world government, a single made-to-order religion: such is the plan of these devils. The Zionists are already preparing their messiah. For them the false-messiah will be king, will rule here on earth." He understood the occult nature of what lies behind many political events, stating that "The Zionists want to rule the earth. To achieve their ends they use black magic and Satanism." He described how the banking system is the means by which Satan will enslave the earth, and that this is the real meaning of "666" in the Book of Revelation. Just as the ancient Hebrews forced those peoples they conquered to pay a tax equivalent of six hundred and sixty-six talents of gold (3 Kings 10 v14 and 2 Chronicles 9 v13), so the one world government will use taxes to dominate the world it has overpowered. Saint Paisios said "The Antichrist wants to subjugate the world using this system. It will be foisted on people with the help of the mechanisms which control the world economy." Those who do not accept the banking mark of 666 will be shut out of all economic life. In unambiguous terms he stated

315

"Behind the credit card system and computerised security lurks worldwide dictatorship and the yoke of the Antichrist."

The war that must occur before the appearance of Antichrist will result in many millions of deaths, he said, and the sign that it is approaching will be the destruction of the Mosque of Omar (The Dome of the Rock in Jerusalem). This will be the sign that the Jews are rebuilding the Temple of Solomon: there are already groups in Israel preparing the priests' vestments and designing the ritual objects. After the war, Saint Paisios prophesied that the Jews will have great power in Europe, and that Christians will suffer terrible persecutions. As a result, those whose faith is shallow will fall away, while the faithful will unite in Orthodoxy as they cling to the truth. The Antichrist will be adept at dividing Christians, and already we see schisms and the threat of schism, and always we find at the root of these Freemasons and those who pursue worldly goals.

Saint Paisios encouraged us to become secure in our faith, to live lives rich in repentance and prayer, and to reject the false illusion of love which leads Christians to accept evil. The world's joys cannot sustain us and will not enable us to reach paradise; if we remain passive we make our enemy stronger and he will be emboldened to attack the truth more openly. All of us must recognise our apocalyptic mission as Orthodox Christians; we each have a responsibility to live a true life of Orthodoxy for the sake of our souls and for the whole world. We must hold tight to the inner conviction that our faith can save us for eternity, and know that no matter how corrupt and powerful the world may be, in the light of Christ's Second Coming the real face of evil will be unmasked. We must not be lulled into imagining we can compromise with the world, in this war there can be no truce: we either conquer or are conquered. Our struggles here in time in this world will determine our eternal condition, and so we must reject the temporary comforts that tempt us from taking up our cross.

Let us open our eyes to what is happening, let us recognise the how Satan is working against us with every weapon his kingdom provides. As Bishop Nektary said before the fall of the USSR, "Soviet Russia already gives us an example of what we may expect – only worse, for the times do not get better." But we must not allow fear to divert us, we follow the King Who is victorious in all things.

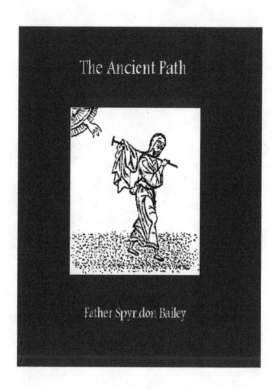

The Ancient Path is a collection of reflections based on quotations from the Fathers of the Orthodox Church. It is available from Amazon and Amazon Kindle.

JOURNEY TO MOUNT ATHOS

FATHER SPYRIDON BAILEY

Journey To Mount Athos describes Father Spyridon's encounters with monks and hermits during a pilgrimage to the Holy Mountain.
See Father Spyridon's author's page on Amazon for more books.

CPSIA information can be obtained
at www.ICGtesting.com
Printed in the USA
LVHW030731200521
687942LV00002B/77